THE ROAD AHEAD

Also by Christabel Bielenberg

THE PAST IS MYSELF

CHRISTABEL BIELENBERG

THE ROAD AHEAD

BANTAM PRESS

LONDON · NEW YORK · TORONTO · SYDNEY · AUCKLAND

TRANSWORLD PUBLISHERS LTD
61–63 Uxbridge Road, London W5 5SA

TRANSWORLD PUBLISHERS (AUSTRALIA) PTY LTD
15–23 Helles Avenue, Moorebank, NSW 2170

TRANSWORLD PUBLISHERS (NZ) LTD
3 William Pickering Drive,
Albany, Auckland

Published 1992 by Bantam Press
a division of Transworld Publishers Ltd

A catalogue record for this book is available from the British Library.

ISBN 0593 02432X

Typeset in 13/14½ pt Garamond medium
by Photoprint, Torquay, Devon

Printed in Great Britain by
Mackays of Chatham plc, Chatham, Kent

Writing is sometimes a curiously lonely occupation, and I am very grateful to my husband, Peter, and also to my now much extended family, all of whom gave me encouragement to carry on. I would also like to thank my publishers for their patience and Antonia Till, whose sensitive editing helped me to finish my self-appointed task.

Contents

Introduction

THE DECISION TO write a
sequel to my original account of my life in Nazi Germany
before and during the Second World War came about because,
after the publication of *The Past is Myself*, I received numerous
letters – in all some four thousand – among which were many
expressing disappointment that, after having become involved
with my family and its story, my readers were left in the air so
to speak, wishing to know what happened to us all afterwards.

I am conscious that some who pick up our story for the
first time may find themselves confused as to how and why
the Bielenberg family, a German husband, his British wife
and their three little boys, aged ten, nine and three at the
time, ended the war in Rohrbach, an isolated little village in
the Black Forest.

For them the explanation would be that, after the failure
of the bomb plot to rid Germany of Hitler which happened
on 20th July 1944, Peter, my husband, was arrested and
spent nearly seven months in Ravensbrück Concentration
Camp. He was released in February 1945 and assigned to
a punishment squad in the Army. He escaped to Rohrbach,
where our sons and I were evacuees from the air raids

over Berlin, and remained there in hiding until the war was over.

In retrospect I am certain that he, perhaps all of us, would never have survived but for the goodness and integrity of those Rohrbach villagers to whom I dedicate this book.

PART ONE

Germany

'In der Heimat, der Heimat, da
gibt's ein Wiederseh'n'
(In the homeland, in the homeland, there we shall meet again)
German soldiers' song

Chapter One

On 20th APRIL 1945 Hitler celebrated his fifty-sixth birthday; ten days later he was dead.

The news reached us as we sat around the stove in the *gute Stube* of the *Gasthaus Adler* listening to the wireless which was our only remaining link with the outside world.

Since the arrival of the French in our little local town of Furtwangen, the Adler had recovered something of its pre-war repute and become once more a rallying point for many bewildered Rohrbach villagers, eager to pick up the latest rumour, eager if possible to hear the latest news, although Frau Muckle's ancient contraption gurgling and whistling away in the corner seemed sometimes as confused as we were as to quite which programmes we were listening to. Allied? German? To which side did all those voices at present belong? Which version were we supposed to believe, as day by day more and more German townships, further chunks of German land were overrun, changed hands and passed under the control of American, British, Russian and French armies?

This time the wireless seemed certain of its message. (There had been plenty of rumours, but this was a certainty.) It gave no details as to where, how and when, but just crackled out something about Hitler (the Führer), having first appointed Admiral Dönitz to be his successor, had made up his mind to die a hero's death and had done so.

A sudden stillness came over the room as the message petered out along with the usual mechanical convulsions. Perhaps even the death of a devil casts a certain spell, for by force of habit some crossed themselves while others just stared at the stove, some took the odd sip from one of the lemonade bottles which Frau Muckle had managed to provide for our entertainment, others puffed on pipes filled with tobacco left behind by the departing German *Wehrmacht*. Only the measured clacking of the cuckoo clock on the wall behind us interrupted the silence.

'*Na*', '*ja*', – so that was it; he was dead. Although Allied bombers still droned occasionally overhead, reminding us that some parts of Germany still had to pass through the final ordeal, he, Hitler, was gone. It could not be long now before the *coup de grâce*, the final knock-out blow, was administered to his mad dream of creating a Thousand Year Reich, empty of all but pure-bred Germans; round blond heads, glowing blue eyes, Aryans one and all – oh dear.

But we, Peter and I, our three sons and the good friends around us were alive, we had outlived him. He had not managed to drag us off with him to some preposterous make-believe Valhalla. So perhaps it was for that reason that the silence was suddenly broken and we found ourselves glancing at each other, pushing back our stools, starting to our feet and moving eagerly from one to the other in order to hold hands, to embrace, to celebrate, one survivor with another.

The day that an armistice was finally declared and hostilities ceased was the first of a sequence of spring days, clear, warm and glorious. The sun shone over the Black Forest, the sky remained blue and cloudless, and, as the last snows retreated, the dark trees standing sentinel on the hilltops took on a softer, misty quality and overnight the cowslips spread over the pastures like carpets of gold.

Until then such cloudless days had been looked upon with

misgiving, but now the blue skies held no menace and it was as if the whole creation was giving thanks that the killing was over, was bent on giving us a reassuring reminder that life must and would go on.

We were surely in need of such reassurance when Father Kunz, the village priest, arranged for a Mass of Thanksgiving to be held in the village church. Some old men long past their prime, some quiet, sad-eyed women and the children; these were the remains of his flock. He doubtless meant it well, but I could not believe them capable as yet of showing much gratitude.

Months had passed since news seeped through from the battlefields. Until then it had been a scribbled note, at most some official flowery account of a brave warrior killed in action whilst defending the Fatherland. But of late the post had brought simply a brief communication telling that a husband or a son was *vermisst*; missing somewhere in those blazing infernos of the eastern or the western battlefronts. At Father Kunz's Mass of Thanksgiving therefore, those who were 'missing' could only take their places in the side chapels as faded, dog-eared, candle-lit photographs, asking dumbly for a prayer that the *barmherzige Gott*, the merciful God, might take pity, and send them home again.

We still had to learn that war loosens its grip only with reluctance. After the *Wehrmacht* left us, no more than three days passed before a little boy in his Sunday best, returning from Mass, spotted a hand-grenade, carelessly discarded by retreating soldiery and wedged into the bank of a tinkling rivulet.

He knew something of warfare, that little boy; his brother was somewhere in France. 'All you have to do is pull the cord and it flies like a butterfly — bangs like a bird scarer!' His name was Hans and he was a schoolfriend of our older sons, Nicky and John, who, along with their other schoolmates, were called to stand guard beside his coffin.

From then on we barely had time to bother about military occupation as we combed the hills, collecting similar lethal trinkets of war from the woods, the streams and the haybarns and stacking them by the roadside. But Peter's dire warnings and even Sepp the cobbler's heavy hand, guaranteed to administer swift punishment to any child failing to give these dumps the widest of berths, could not prevent four further such accidents in the valley.

Our first contingent of liberators consisted of a regiment of French engineers. They were armed to the teeth, but seemed content to rattle through the village by jeep and truckload at breakneck speed, yelling, '*Sale Boche*' at anyone who did not leap for the ditches and doorways with sufficient alacrity.

When they screeched to a halt, it was only to nail placards to the trees informing us of the deeds of valour performed by *La Grande Armée du Rhin et de la Danube*, under the inspired command of General Lattre de Tassigny, and to threaten us with the dire fate which awaited us should we descend to looting, consider disobeying an order, or move further than one kilometre from our homes. We were also instructed to wear white armbands in case we should forget that we had capitulated.

For relaxation, the *Ingénieurs* fished the streams with hand grenades or took pot-shots at the porcelain caps on the telegraph poles, thereby destroying whatever remained of the communication system.

These were followed by the Spahis and then by the Ghoumiers. The Spahis turned out to be bearded Moroccans in white turbans and flowing capes, looking most glamorous and dignified when astride their Arab ponies; but when evening fell they roamed the countryside on foot, searching for food, but, above all, for women. Their first preference was definitely women, but close behind came pigs and also chickens.

The Ghoumiers were small, bow-legged, bearded and slit-eyed. They were dressed in what looked like corduroy dressing-gowns, with ferocious knives stuck through their belts. They moved with uncanny silence on sandalled feet, and they hunted in packs. As far as goals and priorities were concerned, those of the Spahis and the Ghoumiers were identical.

6

The sturdy little peasant girl who had carried the post and who still considered it her duty to report with her empty satchel every morning at Sepp the cobbler-cum-postmaster's shop, was the first victim in our valley. She was discovered lying by the roadside, having been raped so many times that the villagers thought it best to take her to hospital in Furtwangen. Her departure under village escort was the prelude to innumerable sorties which reached their climax when the *Fuchsfallewirt*, an old man living in a remote farmhouse in the upper valley, was shot dead when trying to protect his sixty-seven-year-old wife from a similar fate.

I could not say whether the comparative immunity of the Adler was due to a somewhat unorthodox Union Jack which I chalked on some cardboard and stuck up in the window, but it certainly came from no other form of communication, for these scavengers could speak little French. When, therefore, a terrified squeak from Frau Muckle summoned me to the kitchen door, the resulting conversation was limited.

'You — husband?'

'*Ah oui*, me, big, big husband.'

'Where husband?'

'Husband with *Commandant. Comprenez-vous*, you blighter! *Commandant.*'

A wide sweep of the arm in the direction of Furtwangen and it seemed I had found the magic formula, for thereafter, except for the loss of the odd hen or two, I could reckon on their dejected departure.

News of my successes soon spread up the valley, so that although she could provide nothing to eat or drink, Frau Muckle's *Gaststube* was seldom empty of apprehensive ladies, old and young, seeking the protection of the British flag. Some brought their knitting, some their mending; so that except for the hens which accompanied them in boxes and baskets wherever they went, and were inclined occasionally to lay eggs on the floor, and also the fact that conversation turned mainly towards how best to barricade bedroom doors, we might have been taking part in some pleasantly sociable, non-stop Mothers' Meeting.

Only the official news which reached us over Frau Muckle's ancient wireless reduced us to complete silence, as it told us that Allied troops were overrunning one concentration camp after another, and finding there nothing but half-demented ghostlike caricatures of human beings, together with mounds of neatly stacked skeletal corpses. It also told us of the possibility that not thousands, but hundreds of thousands of Jews, gypsies and dissidents had been systematically put to death in gas chambers.

We were not accustomed to believing a single word delivered to us by the wireless, but this, after all, was no longer Nazi stuff: it was official Allied information. Could it be possible? Any more possible than the unofficial reports brought to us by passing refugees that the Russians were taking their revenge? Raping, looting, burning, driving the fleeing population before them like cattle?

Then all eyes would be turned to me, the *Frau Doktor*, the only possible representative of an Allied power they knew and believed to be trustworthy. I could not be of much help because I, too, was confused, conscious that in my ignorance I had expected far too much, prattled far too confidently of what would follow, of some kind of super-millennium reflecting all the long-lost virtues of liberty and justice. Now that I was confronted with reality, the sheer relief at having survived with my entire family gave way all too rapidly to disillusionment and mounting anger.

Yes, I supposed, these news bulletins, no longer cooked up by Dr Goebbels and his Ministry of Propaganda, but authorized by the Allies, could, certainly should, be authentic. But, as one enormity followed another, such as a camp overseer amusing herself by making lampshades out of human skins, preferably tattooed skins, I began to have serious doubts.

It was the murder of the *Fuchsfallewirt*, a friendly old man trying to pit his feeble strength against the iniquity of power, which succeeded in shaking me out of a mood which was nearing despair. For some reason or other it also roused in me something which in retrospect I could only believe to be a severe attack of rampant chauvinism. I felt myself becoming daily more British; fiercely, uncompromisingly, die-hard British. So much for liberation and all that rubbish. We had merely exchanged the National Socialist German Workers' Party for *La Grande Armée du Rhin et de la Danube*; neurotic Germans for neurotic Frenchmen. As for the French, they had always been, and would always remain, a bunch of egocentric frog-eaters; wogs begin at Calais, a plague on these confounded continentals. Such things were simply not done.

I decided that as I could speak adequate French there must be someone in authority somewhere whom I should contact without delay. To blazes with the General Lattre de something-or-other. Orders or no orders, the time had come for me to get moving, to take to the roads, take to a bicycle, take to any old bicycle – it might even have to be Sepp's bicycle, the only village bicycle about the place since my own and all the others had left home with the *Wehrmacht*.

My departure for Furtwangen was not particularly dignified because Sepp's bicycle had its own ideas on how best to cover the ground. But I managed to concoct another, rather more accurate, facsimile of the Union Jack which I fixed to the handlebars. I was also heartened by assurances from Peter – who did not really approve of the expedition – that if I had not returned by late afternoon, he would take a short cut through the woods, meet me on the road as near to the town as possible and escort me and my virtue safely back home again.

I need have had no fear of meeting up with some prowling Spahi on the main road from Schönenbach to Furtwangen, nor had I time to pay much heed to my dignity nor that of my cardboard flag. The narrow winding highway was alive with traffic. Huge army vehicles and chunky rattletrap jeeps, all 'Made In America', were being driven along with Gallic enthusiasm, at breakneck speed. Some private cars, too, requisitioned by the French or else stolen by Russians and Poles freed from their labours, were keeping pace as best they could, although many were being driven in first gear and some had tyres, some had none. There were plenty of bicycles, too, which must have been handed over to freed Russian farmworkers, most of whom had obviously never ridden on such a contraption before. The result was that parties of cheerful ladies, in a bewildering assortment of scavenged clothing, wobbled perilously towards me from all directions before collapsing in laughing heaps all over the road. I had to laugh with them often enough as I extricated myself from one pile after another of arms and legs and tubular steel for, quite oblivious of the peril they were in, they were enjoying themselves with the infectious abandon of children.

Furtwangen itself resembled a fairground. The pavements were crowded with dazed-looking townsfolk, all obediently wearing their white armbands. The houses in the main street had obviously been taken over by the Russians because each window framed a row of beaming moonlike faces. Radios also facing outwards to the street and, turned on full blast, saw to it that passers-by could be entertained by the resulting ear-splitting din. The hotels, whose decorated walls and flower-bedecked balconies had been a feature of many pre-war travel brochures, were reserved for the Moroccan lady camp-followers. It would seem that, much to the relief of the locals, this most colourful consignment of silks and veils had arrived by the truckload the previous day. Wooden shutters were hastily improvised, they quickly set up shop, and – 'Jesus Maria' – were obviously doing good business behind the unlikely façades of the *Gasthäuser zum Bären, zum Hirsch* and *zum Stern*.

My obvious goal was the *Gasthaus zum Löwen*, the largest and most prominent of inns in the town square. It was draped from gable to ground with Tricolours, the Stars and Stripes and a Union Jack quite as bizarre as my own. A few French soldiers armed with tommy guns, and smoking cigarettes, were lounging about in the sun on the stone steps before the entrance.

Brandishing my version of my national flag, and shouldering Sepp's bicycle, I pushed past them up the steps. I had to think of the anxious eye with which Sepp had watched my departure from Rohrbach, and decided to stow his old bicycle under the stairs before approaching the *gute Stube*, the dining-room, where the door was adorned with a picture of General Lattre de Tassigny, several more Tricolours and the announcement that it was now the office of the Military Commandant. Having got so far, I thought I might just as well push open the door without knocking, and so I disturbed a dark handsome young man in uniform who was examining some papers at one of the tables. The only other person in the room was a well-made blonde who appeared to be his secretary.

'*Bonjour, monsieur*,' I announced rather breathlessly, finding it awkward to slip into a language I had not spoken for years. 'Please excuse the interruption, but I happen to be English, and I feel that I have things to report which could be of interest and some concern to you.'

The young man got to his feet politely and offered me a chair. 'But certainly, madame,' he said, and added, 'this is my secretary, Fräulein G.'

'She speaks French, monsieur?'

'A little.'

I found myself staring intently at Fräulein G. I knew why, and I soon reckoned that she did also. There was no need to go by the book or the badge. After twelve years of Hitler's rule, I would have had to be an imbecile not to recognize a Nazi when I saw one. This specimen oozed National Socialism from the top of her neat blond head to the toe of her patent-leather shoe.

'You learned it in Paris, I suppose?' I remarked mildly, and when she nodded, I added very nastily, 'During the occupation, I suppose? You must have had great fun in Paris, during the occupation, I mean.'

That remark seemed to me so good that I decided to repeat it, nice and slowly, in French.

Capitaine C. was not only handsome but he had an intelligent, sensitive eye, and I was not too surprised when he agreed to speak with me alone.

During the two hours that we sat together that day in

the *Gasthaus zum Löwen*, I became aware of many things, and sensed my rising resentment for our liberators beginning to subside. I even had hope that some of his detestation of *le sale Boche* did likewise. Capitaine C. listened patiently to my accounts of the excesses taking place in his district; he made no denials nor excuses. The colonial troops were splendid in battle, but they lacked experienced officers. He came from an army family. As a cadet in St Cyr, when the German hordes were swarming through his country, he had taken part in that hopelessly heroic cavalry charge on the advancing German tanks, after which there were few left alive to form the nucleus of an officers' corps.

'We behaved as if on parade, wore our white cockaded caps, sheer madness, but we felt at the time we would rather face an honourable death than defeat in dishonour.'

From his father's or grandfather's point of view, the present troops were no French army as they had known it, but an undisciplined rabble, partly genuine Maquis, partly those who joined the bandwagon when they saw which way things were going. Occupation, he believed, corrupted entirely; corrupted the occupiers as well as the occupied. The *Wehrmacht*, the German front-line troops, had behaved well enough at the start in France, but what came after? There were some unsung heroes to be sure, but also secret police, informers, collaborators. '*Ce n'était pas joli, madame – pas joli.*'

Before parting, I asked him whether he thought that the news reaching us by wireless could possibly all be true, and he confirmed my worst fears, telling me simply that after his experience in France, he personally could believe anything.

Capitaine C. helped me down the steps with Sepp's bicycle and we shook hands in parting. I do not think he resented the fact that I had possibly deprived him of a secretary, for he also gave me a permit which allowed Madame Bielenberg to '*circuler à bicyclette*' with the blessings of the Military government, and asked me to report to him should I be in need of any help.

As I wove my way homewards deep in thought, hardly

aware of the crazy circus going on about me, I tried to come to grips with new unaccustomed emotions.

We had opposed; we had lost. The French had lost also; so maybe they had to compensate, had to show now what heroes they were – *La Grande Armée* – clad, fed and set in motion by the Americans or the British. But grandiloquence was in vain for, white armband or no white armband, behind the innocent blue eye of every German man, woman or child they must read or think to read the fateful message: six weeks, it had taken six short weeks to occupy their beloved Paris. They could insult, plunder, rape, even murder – it would take long years, probably a new generation, to wipe out the bitter memory of those six short weeks.

And as for Germany? She had surely lost far more than a war. Millions of her people, her land, her heritage, her honour. With her cities and townships in ruins, it would seem she had lost even her identity. What country could afford such profligacy? Chasing after a myth, a perverse preposterous pie-in-the-sky?

A soft evening mist was rising from the fields as I left the main road behind me and pushed up the hill towards Rohrbach. My bout of chauvinism having subsided, I found myself drained dry, dead weary of this monotonous chorus of failure. I felt no sympathy, no hostility, but just a dull longing to get home. I was merely a pseudo-German and home for me was not Hamburg, not Berlin, not even Rohrbach, but a warm glowing sheltered place, miles away, on an island where I belonged.

A cheerful yodel from near the tree line brought me swiftly back to reality. I had been away over-long. Nicky and John had been sent to keep look-out while Peter prepared to set off for Furtwangen on the short cut through the woods.

In spite of the delight expressed at the successful outcome of my journey, I knew something of the character of my own particular German, and had to wonder whether there was not a slight air of disappointment at my trouble-free, unmolested home-coming. For if he had been called to my rescue,

Peter could have jettisoned so much bottled-up energy, such mounting frustration in one glorious, quite legitimate punch-up with whichever liberator happened to come his way.

In truth, since the inevitable defeat of his country, the daily round had proved almost more difficult for Peter than for me. He could speak no French, so that when army patrols were around rooting out deserters and possible prisoners of war, he was confined to dodging about inside the four walls of the Adler; into the attic, under the hay; the initial thrill of the game could not last for ever. True, he had his release document from Ravensbrück Concentration Camp, but rumour had it that there were so many forgeries in circulation that the Allies were beginning to pay little heed to such things.

I at least could kid myself that I was doing something about it all; he was able to do so only once, when three rugged figures came trudging up the valley and sat themselves down on the bench outside the kitchen door. They could speak little German and wanted to talk with the Bielenberg who was a doctor, and '*oh ja*', if need be they could wait all day. When Peter appeared and sat down with them, after coming back into the kitchen to fetch his bag of *Wehrmacht* tobacco, I felt no shame at listening in to their voices through the open kitchen window above their heads. They were Poles freed from some prison camp near Triberg and they had been told by the authorities that in due course they would be repatriated. But with the passing of the months and the years they had taught themselves to trust no one. They hoped that they still had wives and also children at home, and they wanted advice. Should they wait, or should they scram and risk the long journey back to Poland on their own?

When I heard Peter ask them how it was they trusted him to give them an answer, how indeed they knew his name, they chuckled amongst themselves as a cloud of cigarette smoke drifted past my window. Hadn't he been through the same thing, hadn't he escaped from camp and been hiding in the woods for the last six weeks? There was not a Pole, nor for that matter a Russian, in the district who did not know of it. Who else should they come to but to a fellow fugitive? Peter gave them the best advice he could think of, which was to stay put a little longer as his country was in such turmoil that a journey homewards over hundreds of miles on foot could possibly end in disaster.

It was only after they got up to leave and Peter went with them to the bend in the road and they were shaking hands all round, talking and laughing up at him as they stuffed their pockets with the remains of his tobacco, that it occurred to me that I had learned of a different breed. They had their own secret lines of communication; they had known of Peter's whereabouts, but it had not occurred to any of them to betray him. This was a new kind of brotherhood, with a simple moral code, essential for the survival of those who were up against an unpredictable authority, those who were perforce on the run.

As we sat on the hillside and passed my precious permit from hand to hand, the importance of my being allowed to circulate on a bicycle was not as yet quite clear to any of us. The boys seemed to contemplate with much merriment the possibility of their mother pedalling about the countryside in ever-decreasing circles, whereas Peter and I were not sure whether Sepp's bicycle could make a further trip without collapsing altogether.

In fact my humble slip of paper held other advantages. It signified that I could speak French and had been granted special privileges however limited. With the privileges also came responsibilities, for as soon as the news spread up the valley, a special village bicycle appeared from nowhere and was put at my disposal, nor was it long before Frau Muckle's *gute Stube* was promoted to becoming some kind of miniature Court of Appeal. 'They've taken my last pig, *Frau Doktor*!' – 'I'm down to one hen!' – 'How am I supposed to feed the cow, with no hay left until the harvest?' – these were problems I could not solve, but when Hans Bausch's wife came hotfoot to tell me that Hans had been taken away in the night and that as far as she could understand it had something to do with America, it was easy enough to put two and two together. For it had been simple Hans the milkman who had found an escaping American airman sleeping in the woods and had taken him home, and come to me suggesting I might like to have a chat with him.

My journey to rescue Hans took me as far as Tuttlingen where I finally found him sitting on the hut floor of what was seemingly a collection point for major war criminals. He was crying like a helpless child and told me he thought that they felt he had murdered a *ganzen Haufen* – a whole heap of Americans somewhere between Furtwangen and Villingen.

When he returned home and came to give me some bacon for my pains, I think he still had little idea of the fate which could have befallen him, any more than he or I could have known at the time what had happened to our American airman who, having decided he could run no further and had little chance of crossing the Rhine, was fed and cared for by the villagers and left us under police escort *en route*, as we were still naïve enough to believe, for a prisoner-of-war camp. [1]

But there were also days when I wished I could not speak French. Days when a truckload of assorted 'civilians' would draw up and grind to a halt before the Adler, and an interpreter was needed to sort out the genuine civilians from those who were deserters from the *Wehrmacht* and destined for prisoner-of-war camps.

It was always the same. A row of tired war-weary faces, their expressions alternating between hope and resignation. A cursory inspection could have passed them off as ordinary, somewhat eccentrically clad citizens in ill-fitting clothing, which I knew had been provided by good-hearted householders who had given them temporary refuge. The command to undress never had to be followed further than the shirt or jacket, for underneath was always the rough grey woollen army-issue vest, and that vest sealed their fate.

1 He and his escort were ambushed by storm-troopers between Furtwangen and Villingen and he was shot by order of the local *Kreisleiter* (Party Boss) who was later condemned to death as a war criminal for five other similar offences.

Perhaps soldiers find it hard to discard their few possessions, for once only was I successful in getting my message across: 'Please remember that I am merely here to interpret,' I would pronounce with much solemnity. 'The French officers here can speak no German, and it's your underclothes, your *Unterwäsche* you understand, that they are interested in.' On this one occasion the words were hardly out of my mouth before a skinny little individual in an outsize overcoat, doubled up suddenly clutching his stomach. *'Frau,'* he screamed, his face contorted in pain. *'Frau, ia muess scheisse!'* (I must shit). Bavarian, I could gather and not too easy to translate. But when I explained as best I could to one of the guards that I thought we might be in trouble, as it looked as if this one was going to fill his pants any minute, I met with understanding and he was allowed to retire to our outside lavatory, which was directly above the cesspool under the dung heap.

When some weeks later the pool was drained to spread its contents on the meadows, it did not really surprise anyone that the pipes were almost choked with what still resembled a vest, some long underpants and a pair of woolly socks.

The true significance of my visit to Capitaine C. in Furtwangen emerged only later when a vehicle drew up outside the Adler, and there was a knock on the front door. Peter for the hayloft, ladies beware, hens away, I went to open up prepared to recite my usual dogmatic gibberish: 'Big, big husband, *Commandant*, *Angleterre*, *Allez*! *Allez!*' Whenever I think of the sight which met my eyes when I opened that back door, it comes back to me with all the vividness of divine revelation.

The uniform was British, the beret was British, the short leather-covered swagger-stick stuck under the arm was British, and the words, 'Excuse me, Captain Register's my name, SHAEF British American liaison 6th French army. Sorry to bother you, but I heard over in town there was a British woman living here somewhere, and we thought – we might – we could . . .'

We? I glanced behind him to where two further archangels

were clambering out of an army jeep flying the Tricolour and also a real Union Jack. "Ullo, Mum,' said one; and, 'Good day, missus,' said the other as they came towards me. Came towards me and came to a dead stop, as well they might, because the 'British woman living here somewhere' had found nothing better to do than burst into a torrent of uncontrollable tears.

When Captain Register and his companions drove off three hours later, awash with watery coffee and well supplied with the hunks of fat bacon which Frau Muckle insisted was absolutely necessary to keep soldiers on the go, they left us with many valuable gifts, perhaps the most priceless being the careful and sympathetic heed they paid to our story and the effort they made to understand.

I could write my first letter to my parents in six years, telling them of our survival and begging for news. Peter could unburden himself of at least some of the confused emotions fermenting in his mind: his certainty that it would not be long before hunger spread disease, and that the children and I should be spared; his own helplessness in a zone where he could not speak the language of authority; the sense of responsibility inherent in having survived and his own wish to be of use somewhere in his demoralized and defeated country.

As for the children - manna from heaven! They could be introduced to two oranges, one banana and three whole bars of Cadbury's chocolate.

Captain Register's parting gift was a singularly unconventional document, written in ink on one of my remaining pieces of notepaper, wherein he, Captain Register of British American 6th Army group, SHAEF, introduced Peter Bielenberg of German extraction and his wife, British born, the daughter of Lieutenant-Colonel Burton of the British army and requested assistance for them in any way possible.

He handed it over to us with a grin, saying that it might help, but he wished he had had some kind of a rubber stamp with him as in any army there were few things so useful as a bloody impressive-looking rubber stamp.

Although we did not realize it, he was providing us

with the equipment needed for the start of a long odyssey which would include our bidding farewell to Rohrbach and would end . . . Well, where would it end? We had no idea at the time but when we parted they left behind a miniature hive of industry and ingenuity. Did someone mention something about the occupation corrupting? What about that Citroën which must have been requisitioned by the *Wehrmacht* in France, and abandoned in the ditch before being rescued and hidden in the village bowling-alley before the French arrived? It probably only needed petrol to get it on the road again and with a bit of luck some of those wrecked hulks of *Wehrmacht* lorries lying about in the fields might still have a few cupfuls of fuel in their tanks. All that was needed was a hammer, a nail and a bucket, and Peter and the boys would soon find out.

Had Captain Register not mentioned something too about rubber stamps? What better than that of the Military Governor of the district? We'd have to drive to Villingen, twenty-eight kilometres, on one bucket of petrol. There would also be military patrols on the road, but Peter and I both had green-grey anoraks, not dissimilar to those of French army issue and being as brown as a berry from the waist up, at least Peter could be mistaken for a deaf and dumb Frenchman or even a Moroccan. What I could be mistaken for would be anyone's guess!

Our journey was completely successful. We dodged past three patrols, saluting smartly and stepping equally smartly on the accelerator, and arrived in Villingen to discover that Capitaine Robert was an extremely civilized, very confused, Military Governor. His father had been a diplomat in London and he spoke excellent English. Due to the antics of the *Ingénieurs* with the telegraph wires, he was also extremely isolated, and showed his gratitude for the information we could give him about his district by providing Captain Register's document with two quite splendid rubber stamps. Our world was expanding by the day. We could now travel by any means at our disposal to Stuttgart *et retour*. Although the means at our disposal were one stolen motor car and one decrepit bicycle, Peter decided blithely that nothing less than a motor bicycle would suit his requirements.

As communication by post or telephone was prohibited for German citizens, he must get to Hamburg and reassure his mother that he was still alive; he must get himself a job; he must look for Clarita, the widow of Adam von Trott, a great friend of ours, who had been cruelly executed after the failure of the 1944 Plot against Hitler's life. Peter wanted to see if he could be of help to her. His spirits were high and his plans were boundless; all he needed was that motor cycle. Rumour had it that there was a warehouse packed with requisitioned vehicles somewhere on the other side of Furtwangen so, armed with our document, off he went through the woods and returned in the evening astride a magnificent machine which looked as if it had barely left the assembly line.

He threw caution to the winds and wasted some of our precious petrol careering about the forest tracks with the boys riding pillion before setting off on what must have been a unique journey: from our south-west corner of what remained of his country, through all three occupied zones across the River Elbe to Hamburg. He returned three weeks later, his mission accomplished, having proved Captain Register's theory to be correct, for our ridiculous document now had a collection of rubber stamps fit to be framed.

Before the war ended a joke was doing the rounds about a citizen saying to his friend that when the war was over he intended to make a bicycle tour all round Germany, and his friend replied by asking him what he was going to do in the afternoon!

In fact no one seemed to know exactly what would be left of Germany, what indeed had been decided in Yalta when Churchill, Roosevelt and Stalin had divided the spoils and carved out the territories over which they would hold sway when victory was theirs. In Hamburg it was known that to the east, in Schleswig-Holstein, huge prisoner-of-war camps were being run with much efficiency by officers of the German *Wehrmacht*. Why? Could it mean that at least the British had woken up to the fact that although the Nazi menace was now behind them, the barbarous advance of the Russians into Europe might not bode too well for the future?

But for us in Rohrbach it was the present which occupied our minds. Peter had found his family alive; hungry, but well. Clarita, also, had been freed from prison, but was not yet reunited with her children who, after Adam's death and her own imprisonment, had been removed from their grand-mother's care and placed in a Nazi children's home.

Frankfurt had become the headquarters of the American zone of occupation, and because of his clean sheet politically and his newly found ability to communicate, Peter had found himself a job in the recently established Chamber of Commerce. He must leave again at once, for there was even the possible chance that two or three rooms in a little house in Kronberg, just outside the town, might be put at his — at our — disposal.

After he left again, I was overtaken by increasing restlessness, persuading myself that there was little more I could do to help.

Lush weeds and wild raspberry canes were beginning to camouflage the rusting war machines which still littered the meadows; one such monster had been taken over already by a little bird, busy building its nest in the exhaust pipe. There would surely always be the odd crisis but life in the valley would go on, could go on, without me.

I was also unhappy as I had had no reply to my message to my family. Perhaps Frankfurt would be more central, perhaps I should try from there. Indeed I had sent off two messages into the blue, the second by way of a gay Irishman who appeared on the scene not only bent on having a good time but, seeing that he was in the logging trade in Canada, also to cast a curious, perhaps even covetous, eye over the acres of massive conifers known as the Black Forest.

'You will have to leave us one day, *Frau Doktor*.' Frau Muckle gave a loving glance at Christopher who was sitting on her lap having his supper. She had become as devoted to

Christofli as to a grandson. 'You will have to leave us and I — we — will wish you Godspeed, but we will miss you here in the valley.'

So it was to be. A further trip to Frankfurt riding pillion on Peter's motor cycle, a cursory inspection of some small empty rooms in a little house in Kronberg, and a return journey to Rohrbach at the wheel of an elderly motor car, the registered property of the Frankfurt Chamber of Commerce.

On the eve of our departure, I could hear unusual stirrings in the *gute Stube* next door to our little sitting-room, which looked strangely forlorn after I had taken down our two pictures and rolled up the rug. At breakfast Frau Muckle had mentioned rather over-casually that some of the villagers might want to drop in that evening to say goodbye, for if I was leaving at dawn the following day they might be held up at home with the cows and so on.

When Sepp's two daughters joined her and Martina in the kitchen though, to spend the afternoon bustling back and forth at her bidding, and I also heard her rummaging about in the chimney where she hid the smoked meats, I had to suspect that something rather out of the ordinary might be afoot.

I was packing all day, trying to figure out which of our few possessions we could discard in order to cram children and dire necessities into the motor car, so that dusk was moving up the valley before I glanced out of the window to see Sepp and his wife emerging from their shop and approaching the front entrance to the Adler. They were both dressed as if for Mass and Sepp had his hat on. A further glance down the road and I could distinguish the mayor's bread-van approaching from the direction of Schönenbach and across the valley quite a few black-clad figures seemed to be converging on the inn.

I had a dress somewhere in one of the bundles and hurried upstairs to drag it out. The boys were over-excited and had been a nuisance all day, but at least they should be clean.

Frau Muckle was quite pink with excitement when she came to call us, and she had every reason to be so for the *gute Stube* was a festive sight. Many of the tables were spread with

22

white table-cloths, two candles were lit before the statue of the Virgin and Child in the *Herrgottseck* – God's corner – and there were jam-jars of wild flowers in the windows. There had surely been nothing like it since we entertained our American airman.[1]

The Rohrbach villagers were standing about in silent groups, not yet quite at ease wearing their Sunday best on a weekday, and as we were ushered in, the Mayor stepped forward, clearing his throat as if to make a little speech. He seemed to change his mind when the *Lehrer* Lorenz and his wife, closely followed by Father Kunz, slipped through the heavy curtainings which covered the front door.

I thought I knew perhaps why. Only three weeks before, I had managed to persuade the Military governor in Villingen to reinstate him as Mayor of Rohrbach in spite of the fact that he had been a member of the Party; a privilege of which he had made no use whatsoever. However, since his world at present was standing on its head, he might have wondered whether the priest should take precedence on such an occasion.

The silence which followed his hesitation could have become oppressive if Martina had not saved the situation by getting a splendid fit of the giggles. She was reprimanded as usual most vehemently by Frau Muckle and as usual took no notice whatsoever, so that our festive array and the mayor's speech were quickly forgotten and we all started talking at the same time before turning our attention to the feast which had been prepared for us.

Something untoward might prevent Frau Muckle from ever entertaining on such a scale again, but now she was bent on doing us proud: two great tureens of steaming noodle soup, a mound of fat smoked bacon and dozens of bottles of fizzy lemonade. We guessed that the three giant loaves which occupied a table all to themselves were a contribution from the mayor's bread-van.

As the meal progressed and we had drained the soup tureens

1 See *The Past is Myself*.

and were well on the way to demolishing the mountain of fat bacon, Sepp made sure of the success of my send-off by telling his daughters to fetch over a bottle or two of his homemade red-currant Schnapps known far and wide to be delicious and quite lethal. As most of us through necessity had become unaccustomed to alcohol of any kind for years, a thimbleful of this heady brew was enough to have us all laughing and talking at the tops of our voices. Hardship and the sorrow of parting were temporarily forgotten as earthy jokes and way-out stories did the rounds in a dialect which became increasingly incomprehensible.

Frau Muckle was asleep behind the stove with Christopher curled up in the log-basket at her feet when the cuckoo clock on the wall told us in staccato style that it was midnight. The last to leave took their plates to the kitchen where Martina was already busy tipping the remains into the pig bucket.

'Goodnight, *Frau Doktor!*'

'God bless you, *Frau Doktor!*'

'Come back soon, *Frau Doktor!*'

'Oh, I will, I will, very, very soon – I promise.'

As I stood in the doorway and watched them disappear into the darkness, although I knew in my heart that a chapter of my life had come to a close, I do not think that I was consciously avoiding the truth.

At five o'clock the next morning, when the summits of the black hills were already outlined against a soft yellow glow and a mist hid the lowlands, we climbed into our little motor car which was barely recognizable beneath the bags and bundles tied to its mudguards and the bulging rug strapped to its roof.

A slight hold-up, and it was fortunate that three sturdy villagers were already up and about, for we had to be pushed for several hundred yards before the engine sprang to feeble life.

Then we were off: Frankfurt, England, here we come! I could not wave goodbye as I needed both hands on the steering-wheel to keep us on the road, but the boys kneeling on the back seat told me that they could still see two white handkerchiefs fluttering bravely, before we rounded a bend in the road and the village hidden behind the morning mist was no longer in sight.

Chapter Two

Nearly four months passed before a Royal Air Force plane of Transport Command took off from the United States Airbase Frankfurt/Main; 'Operation Woman and Child' and Nicholas, John, Christopher and I were airborne *en route* for England.

During those four months we became crafty and self-centred, no different from any others who were being classified by Americans, re-educated by the British, conquered – however belatedly – by the French, while our sole interest lay in planning where the next meal, the next lump of coal, might come from.

Our journey from Rohrbach had taken us many long hours, mastering what remained of Germany's road network. Our maximum speed was a sedate twenty-five kilometres an hour, as, with more skill than sense, I managed to avoid mighty bomb craters which could have swallowed us altogether, and to get ourselves sucked along in the wake of one of the huge army vehicles which seemed to be the only other form of transport on the move. Jeeps and trucks, tanks and gun carriages; when they thundered past us these juggernauts covered us with dust, loosened the ropes and played havoc with the bundles tied to our roof and mudguards. But our little motor car survived and reached its destination, although towards the end of its ordeal it looked no better than a junk heap on wheels.

I had not known Frankfurt before the war, but could imagine that the old part of the town sloping down to the River Main and known as the *Goethe Stadt* might have been beautiful before it was obliterated by bombs. The rest of the city, where it was still intact, seemed merely a faded monument to past prosperity and lack of taste, and the pot-holed streets and pitted pavements did nothing to improve its image.

A large residential area had been cordoned off and the houses requisitioned for occupation troops. It was carefully guarded with a high wire fence and numerous military check-points in order to keep out possible intruders and also disease, about which the Americans seemed to have an almost pathological horror. It was known to the liberated as the 'Ami Ghetto'.

The American GIs, some black, some white, were fine-looking, loose-limbed, young fellows who seemed to spend much of their day squatting on the kerbside chewing gum and casting longing eyes in the direction of any presentable but officially unavailable *Fräulein* who happened to pass by. *Fräuleins* were officially unavailable because after hostilities ceased, the Allies, in their wisdom, had promulgated various directives in the simple hope of solving the immediate problem of how to deal with a race of defeated Germans who had committed unspeakable crimes and yet to meet with, seemed so helpful, so eager to please, so wishful to learn whatever language was required and to insist that, of course, they had never been Nazis and had known nothing of what had gone on during the twelve long years of Hitler's rule.

The only relics of an army which had rampaged through Europe and penetrated deep into Russia were now lonely, silent figures in tattered uniforms, leaning on makeshift crutches or propped up in sheltered doorways. These were the *Schwerkriegsverletzen*, the severely war wounded. The fact that they were legless, armless or blind was surely proof enough, but the rough message chalked on cardboard and the begging

27

bowl on the pavement before them told passers-by that they were also penniless and hungry.

Non-fraternization, a ruling ignored by the Russians and the French, stipulated that unless on official business, no Allied personnel must communicate in any way with a German civilian; no greeting, no word, no smile must be exchanged with any remnant of the once all-conquering Master Race. Every possible contingency had been considered and provided for in order to impress on the Germans that this time they had been truly defeated, and that their behaviour had been beneath contempt. But one all-important factor had not been considered and that was human nature, so, in spite of the presence of quantities of military police, it was not long before a flourishing black market developed in the red-light district near Frankfurt's main railway station; a hive of clandestine activity where alcohol and cameras, fountain-pens and *Fräuleins*, could be bartered for cigarettes and petrol, candies and cookies. Anything for anything, indeed, in a world where life had been reduced to the basics.

We were luckier than most in not having to join the long queues for housing, because Peter had managed to rent three rooms for us in the tiny house in Kronberg, a suburb of Frankfurt. He had also rustled up four beds, a table and some chairs. We had a kitchen with a sink and a stove, and an outside lavatory of the chain-pulling variety. A saucepan, which unfortunately had a habit of turning somersaults, completed the picture. What more could we want? ('Count your blessings, dear' was one of my grandmother's pious maxims if, as children, we ran to her in the belief that life had given us a particularly hard knock.) All right, there was of course much more to want, and there were moments when I almost succeeded in understanding that satisfaction with one's lot is purely a matter of perspective, of comparability. In the Black Forest, there had been times of loneliness, and of despair. I also had to admit to moments of intense boredom when, lying in bed at night, listening to the wind howling over the hills, I sensed with dull resignation that life was passing me by. But we had been sheltered there, cared for by good and simple people and we had also been safe from the bombs. Here in Kronberg we were falling over each other, making do, shuffling along in endless queues for food by day, confined by the curfew to our cramped quarters at night. But, unlike so many others, we were alive, healthy and together, and we had a roof over our heads.

The rumour of that roof over our heads soon spread, so that homeless friends appeared out of the blue, certain of welcome and a chance to sleep somewhere on a nice dry floor. Freda Winckelmann was one of the first to arrive and became a permanent fixture. I was delighted to see her because though I longed to leave for England, I suffered an occasional twinge of conscience as to what would happen to Peter after I had left, and here was one of my closest friends who would be the perfect candidate to take my place.

Freda and her husband Hannes Winckelmann were long-standing friends from Hamburg. We had married in the same year, but they were both older than ourselves and, much to Freda's sadness, they had no children.

Hannes was by profession a not very successful lawyer, by temperament probably an academic. His purpose in life seemed to revolve around some thesis on the subject of Max Weber, an eminent sociologist, which, with the years, was becoming a huge tome. He had also been a friend of Dr Goerdeler, former Mayor of Leipzig, one of the senior members of the Opposition, at whose request he had found himself appointed to a minor post in the Ministry of the Interior in Berlin in order to establish contact there with others of like mind. Needless to say, he was a dedicated anti-Nazi, but if I were to be honest, anyone who cared nothing about Herr Max Weber could find Hannes something of a bore.

Freda came from an estate in East Germany and unlike most other Prussian nobility whose female offspring were driven to learn the art of housekeeping the hard way, her family, the von Rechenbergs, had never insisted on her doing anything at all except enjoy herself, until they lost all their possessions after the First World War. She then had to do something about earning her living and had battled along fairly successfully as a secretary, until finally employed by Furtwängler, the conductor of the Berlin Philharmonic Orchestra.

The longer our friendship lasted, the more certain I became that her success as a secretary was due more to her personality than to her skill with a typewriter. If I needed convincing I only had to go with her to one of the orchestra's rehearsals, and see for myself how she seemed to take each one of those magnificent musicians, including their conductor, under her wing.

Freda was small and wiry, with blue eyes which were inclined to glance at you occasionally with the sparkle of a bright-eyed bird. Her capacity as a listener was limitless, and such was her sympathetic involvement in the affairs of others that if the occasion arose she could burst with laughter, but also, with equal facility, shed a sudden tear.

Just before the Russians arrived in Berlin, a *Luftmine* – an air mine – landed in the Winckelmanns' garden, and successfully flattened their little house in Gatow. She and Hannes had miraculously survived in the cellar, but, homeless and destitute, she had been persuaded to leave for Bavaria with Furtwängler and his orchestra who seemed unable to come to any decision without her. Hannes, still hopeful of the earlier arrival in Berlin of the Americans or the British, preferred to stay at his post in the Ministry. When she heard about our 'roof' in Kronberg she decided to trek westwards and arrived on our doorstep with the remains of her possessions strapped to her back in a rucksack – a few pieces of jewellery, some bundles of old curtains and an equally elderly bedspread which seemed an odd collection until she explained with a confidence which might have been bravado that, since she had no money and no one had much to wear these days, she had decided to turn her hand to dressmaking.

Dear Freda! Neither Peter nor I could remember her being able to darn a sock, or fry an egg for that matter, but even if the mind boggled at the thought of her brave venture into the world of *haute couture* — picturing the trail of chintz and damask sacks liable to fall to pieces at any moment that she might have left behind her *en route* — we had not the heart to dampen her spirit.

Freda was followed by two eminent but rather tiresome professors of Philosophy, mutually good friends until they had to decide who was the more eminent, who indeed deserved the only blanket we could provide for their comfort. The argument as to their respective scholastic merits went on into the early hours until Peter decided that the children were not quite warm enough and removed the blanket leaving the eminent professors to argue themselves to sleep on two very uncomfortable chairs.

I soon learned that in circumstances of need, certain minor moral principles can no longer be relied upon and finally slip away altogether. It was, for instance, surprising how rapidly I switched from being slightly shocked to being simply delighted when the children turned up for lunch waving a piece of chocolate or a banana which could only mean that they had been begging outside the local GI encampment.

Nor did a conversation with my neighbour in one of the food queues in any way reduce my suspicion that the German *Hausfrau* belonged to a very special breed, possibly more dedicated, indomitable and tenacious than the whole of the German and Allied armies rolled into one.

'It was all because of the sugar for the preserves,' she remarked suddenly, as her eyes followed a group of GIs who happened to be passing by.

'*Ja, ja*, of course, the sugar for the preserves . . .' I had no idea what she was talking about but decided that under the circumstances any sort of conversation would do.

'It's the bottled plums,' she went on. 'The syrup, you understand, it needs so much sugar to get them right.'

'Surely,' I said, still well out of my depth until she added, 'He was a nice gentleman, could not speak much German, not black of course, and he never left without paying — a kilo of sugar, sometimes even two — a most satisfactory arrangement.'

My neighbour did not look promiscuous: homely in fact, but also determined and rather pleased with herself.

'Yes, I guess it was a very good arrangement,' I replied as we moved a few steps nearer to the grocer's shop, and for some reason or other I felt myself to be rather inadequate, a truly feeble votary to the goddess of the store cupboard.

It was perhaps this cosy chat which drove me to embark on an expedition which could have ended in disaster. A good friend, the doctor's wife, pretty, respectable, devoted mother to her children, came by with the proposition. She had bicycled to the country with a piece of jewellery and returned with six bottles of wine; not very good wine, she assured me, but she'd heard the *Amis* didn't know the difference. She had also learned that the going rate for wine was two bottles for one jerrycan of army petrol. She had done some reconnoitring and discovered that the guards who took over at our local army camp at night were very partial to the odd bottle of wine. There had to be two of us though, one to keep the guards happy and the other to fetch the petrol from the huge army storage compound some two miles away. Think of it, two whole jerrycans of petrol! Who knows where we could go from there: petrol to cigarettes, cigarettes to butter, butter to — we could end up living on beefsteaks for weeks, and just in case I might be disturbed by anything resembling a still, small voice, she added that it need not mean only food, for we might also pick up some unobtainable medicines *en route*.

The whole expedition had obviously been planned most carefully, for as soon as we arrived at the camp and my friend had jumped out of the car with far more confidence than I knew she possessed, a uniformed figure emerged from under some trees and climbed in beside me. He was bulky and black. 'Howdy, ma name's Louis,' he whispered in an accent coming from well south of the Potomac.

'Howdy, mine's Chris,' I replied and, 'Get going, honey' came his swift reply.

So get going I did, out onto the main road, heading for a glow on the skyline which I knew to be the floodlit petrol compound. Louis was friendly and chatty and it was obviously not the first time that he had set off on such an expedition, for just before we reached the high wire fence topped with barbed wire he told me to stop, waited for two cars to pass us and then—

'Now, Chris, honey, sharp to the right and turn out the lights.'

'Honey' by this time was ready for anything; sharp to the right, the lights were out, and she could see nothing whatsoever. As far as she was concerned we might have been taking a dive into the ocean. But it seemed we had landed on a well-worn trail, and my little motor car had dropped into two deep tracks which allowed no room for manoeuvre. Onwards for about three hundred yards, then Louis patted my knee, told me I had done fine, ordered me to stop and said he would be back in about five minutes.

The five minutes seemed rather long, because although a high bank topped with some kind of a hedge hid the glow of the arc lights to my left, to my right must have been an open field and I could not understand how the headlights from the cars passing along the main road and temporarily lighting up the surrounding countryside did not include me in their vision. A certain amount of rustling and grunting, and Louis was back, dragging two splendid jerrycans of petrol which he stowed on the back seat and we set off on our return journey; in reverse this time, but the tracks still held us on course.

All was going well, in fact I was beginning to enjoy myself when, after we had covered about a hundred yards, a gasp and then a moan from Louis told me that something was definitely not in order.

'Ma luger, doggone it, ma luger, ah've left it in the hedge,' he wailed, and when I turned to look at him, he was no longer the cheerful confident guide, but a heap of misery with nothing much to be seen of him but the whites of his eyes.

'Couldn't we leave it there?' I murmured, not quite certain whether a luger was a pistol or even a machine-gun.

'You jes don't know Uncle Sam,' he replied, and before I could say more he was out of the car, stumbling off back down the track and had disappeared into the darkness, leaving me crouched over the steering-wheel, woefully considering the extent of my misdemeanours and totting up the inevitable consequences. The minutes ticked away, as the headlights from the main road, so much closer now, flashed and faded over my head. It was too much to hope that a passing vehicle would not be alerted: brakes would be applied, huge headlights would swing around and a jeep most likely loaded with military police would draw up behind me and my cargo of contraband loot.

Caught red-handed abroad without permission after curfew, in possession of two jerrycans of stolen army gasoline. With luck, poor Louis crawling about in the hedgerows looking for his luger might make a getaway, otherwise the two of us could look forward to spending part of our lives behind bars, getting to know Uncle Sam.

I had lost count of time when the car door was wrenched open and Louis was back again, sweating and breathless.

'Sweet Jesus,' he gasped as he flung himself down beside me. 'Sweet Jesus, Chris honey, ah found it, ma old luger, ma dear li'l ol' luger.' The words were hardly out of his mouth before our little car started shaking as if overtaken by an earthquake, for Louis had his luger, Louis was a man again, rocking back and forth in a giant fit of uncontrollable laughter.

The remainder of our trip was comparatively uneventful, except that when we arrived back at the camp I could see that my poor friend had not had an easy time either.

'Heavens, Chris!' she exploded as she jumped for the car. 'Whatever happened to you? I reckoned on half an hour at the most, and you've been gone more than two hours — oh dear, what's the English for *hau ab* anyway?'

'Buzz off,' I obliged, and as we headed for home and family, I told her and she told me and we both decided that we were not the stuff of which gun-runners are made. As far as we were concerned, once this consignment was used up, our children could go on eating groats for every meal and our husbands go about their respective businesses on foot.

It was here though, in our little house in Kronberg, that my spirits soared sky-high, for a message reached me from UNRRA (United Nations Relief and Rehabilitation Agency) that my family in England were all alive and well. My brothers Basil and John had survived the African campaign, although for the last two years John had been a prisoner of war, captured after the landing in Italy. My sister and her family had spent the war in Australia and then in Canada. All were heading for home and my father was pulling strings and making arrangements for us to join them as soon as possible.

The silence from the other side was broken; somehow one or other of my many messages must have slipped through the dense wall of censorship. My family had our address and the strings being pulled must have been considerable because close upon that first message followed an invitation from General Morgan of UNRRA for Peter and me to join him for dinner in Kronberg Castle, which was now Allied Command Headquarters. Out with my pre-war blue, my one remaining glad rag, and we were fetched by an army driver in a real motor car, later to dine off real plates and be served real food by real batmen in white jackets. There was silver, there was glass, and the port did the rounds under the cool indifferent eyes of former Princes of Hessen assembled about us in portraits on the walls. But Peter and I knew that what we needed, above all, was the sympathy we received and the interest shown, and the fact that we could take part in serious discussion as to how, after the devastations of war, new structures for Europe must emerge, ensuring that the peoples, currently buffeted about like human driftwood, could reach home, some longed-for harbour, and be allowed to start life anew.

Two evenings later we were paid a surprise visit by several more junior members of General Morgan's staff. They came because they had felt we were of similar age, that British or German we had all perforce grown up under the threatening shadow of an impending world war and it was up to us, to our generation, to see that it never happened again. There was so much more to discuss and they felt we had not reached enough conclusions in the more formal atmosphere of Kronberg Castle.

They knew of our children and, besides three bottles of whiskey, had brought with them a bulging rucksack filled with unheard-of delicacies: chocolates and fruit, sweets and biscuits, even some chewing gum, so we decided that the boys should also have their party. 'Eat yourselves sick,' I chirruped recklessly as they dragged the rucksack back to their bedroom, and when in the early hours of the morning we settlers of the world's ills staggered in to bid them good night, it was obvious that they had taken my advice. Orange peels and banana skins, half-eaten chocolate bars and sweet papers were strewn all over the room with riotous abandon and our sons had passed out, their night-clothes and their peaceful faces smeared with chocolate and aglow with what I hoped was not violent indigestion.

My last official encounter before we left for England was less encouraging. In a way it was brought about by the visit of the UNRRA officers, for the evening had revived so many memories, of times with friends who were no longer alive, of the plans we had made, of the things that must be done. This left me with a guilty conscience, telling myself that in times like these, counting my blessings and cursing the somersaulting saucepan were useless occupations and that I could and should do better. Now that Freda was installed and could look after the children, I was free to take on some kind of job, perhaps as an interpreter. I could, after all, speak three languages fluently and had learned when living in the French zone how the language barrier can impede progress. Here in the American zone many of the officials in the Press and Information and also Intelligence Departments were German-Jewish emigrants who, as Peter had discovered, could speak better German than English, but whose attitude, policies and behaviour understandably made for little positive collaboration. A neutral interpreter then, that's what was needed, and I decided with much confidence that I was made for the job.

The four stalwart guards who stood sentry outside the entrance to the British Liaison Office were easy to deal with, the prescribed rigidity of their facial expressions relaxing immediately to become broad grins on being spoken to by a civilian whose accent they could recognize as the genuine article. From there I progressed from one office to the next and thought I was doing very well until I reached the top, where the interview was short and not very sweet.

'You are British born, I understand, and married to a German – Bylenberg I note – and you wish to enter Allied employment, is that it?'

The gentleman was not very tall, he had a rather steely eye beneath bushy black eyebrows and what remained of his face was hidden behind an outsize moustache.

'Yes, well I suppose it is – er . . .' I got no further.

'Well, I can tell you right away, Frau Bylenberg,' he snapped, 'you have not got a hope.' Whereupon, drawing himself up to his full five foot six, looking almost as if he was about to blow his moustache at me, he added, 'It is my considered opinion that you were a poor fool to marry a bloody German anyway, and . . .'

Whatever he wanted to say next was aimed at a closed door, but fate was to decide that we should meet again under very different circumstances, of which I must tell later.

Down at the entrance the four guards were anxious to know how I had got on, and when I told them that I had been given the thumbs down in no uncertain terms, they were most sympathetic.

'The trouble is that little men never really like tall girls very much,' I found myself confiding rather miserably.

'You look all right to me, miss,' one of them remarked, and seeing that they were all well over six feet, we found ourselves bursting with laughter together, which did much to cheer my dejected frame of mind.

At last the day arrived when an official-looking document required us to report at the Airbase, prepared to take off for London.

We had made two false starts before, and twice taken tearful farewells of Peter at the Airbase entrance check-point, only to spend the rest of the day stuffing doughnuts in a canteen, to be sent home again in the evening like unwanted cargo. On this occasion though we had barely said goodbye when a loudspeaker crackled out our names and we were hustled along several narrow passageways out onto the wide expanse of tarmac. A short jeep ride and we were dumped beside a huge silent grey-green monster. A monster for me, as I had only seen its like before when, together with hundreds of its kin, it winged its way high above the Black Forest *en route* for Augsburg or Munich — towns already shattered, but doubtless preparing to batten down again and dig in once more, awaiting its arrival.

The only other passenger in the same category as ourselves was a pale-faced German girl clutching a brand new British passport and holding a sleeping baby on her lap; the baby was jet black. She could speak no English, and she was scared, she came from near Leipzig and had married an African prisoner of war. The Russians, you see, and, oh yes, he was very kind and had given her food and cigarettes. Did I know Africa? Would he come to meet her? He had not yet seen his son.

As she unburdened herself in obvious relief at finding someone who spoke her own language, my eye wandered from one to the other of my own children. Nicky was holding tightly to a small cardboard suitcase containing the remains of his favourite possessions, Christopher to a coloured handkerchief to which he had become attached, and John had a canvas camera case slung round his neck. It contained my old Box Brownie camera, a birthday present, and I had only been able to keep a flicker of interest in it alive by telling him of the wonderful pictures he would be able to take in England as soon as he could get a film for it.

One of the soldiers was making himself popular by showing

them how to inflate their life-jackets, and when they turned and laughed back at me over their bulging rubber waistcoats, looking for all the world like three bright-eyed coconuts, I decided Peter and I had reason to be proud, for they looked healthy enough in spite of those last months spent in Frankfurt.

'I'm hungry,' Christopher announced at the top of his voice in broad Black Forest dialect. I knew this could not be the case, because even in the short while we had spent in the PX canteen, the Americans had been generous in plying us with food, milk and coffee.

'You'll have to wait until we get to England,' I said firmly, wondering in fact just how long that would be as we were so obviously still rooted to the ground. But Christopher knew better. He eyed John's camera case expectantly, while John, with a slow secret smile, started fiddling with the clasp and finally slipped back its canvas cover. The case no longer housed my Box Brownie and I could only think it had been left on the counter of the PX canteen, for instead, squeezed in most carefully without a square inch to spare, were three neat rows of golden-brown dough-nuts.

Seated to my left was a boy who did not seem inclined to join in the general high spirits. Instead, after apologizing and pushing along the bench to give me more room, he sat there beside me, elbows on knees, quietly reading a book.

Perhaps it was the contrast between the clamour about us and his stillness which made me look at him more closely. Although his trousers were airforce blue, he was not wearing battle-dress, but an old tweed jacket, a blue open-necked shirt and some kind of a silk scarf which did not look like army issue. His face, too, seen in profile, was of a type which I had not seen for many years. My mother, with true British reasoning, always insisted that Germans were pale because they slept with their windows shut. Be that as it may, it was not the fine head, the short straight nose, the crop of curly fair hair, but the rosy freshness of his complexion which made me come to the conclusion that he could not be anything but British and that he was really much too young to have taken part in any war.

Now, as if conscious of my attention, he straightened suddenly and putting aside his book turned to me and smiled. 'Sorry,' he said, 'but you have me puzzled – what nationality are you?'

I had been asked that question many times before. The last time was nine months earlier – it seemed a lifetime ago – on a long train journey back from Berlin to the Black Forest after seeing Peter in Ravensbrück Concentration Camp. The question had come from a pale-faced SS officer, who had slaughtered Jews, who could not forget and who wished in his turn to die.[1] What nationality was I? There was something rather shy and very engaging about my neighbour's smile which made me smile back.

'Well, officially I think I must be a Kraut,' I said and watched his smile broaden immediately.

'I see,' he said, and then with his eye on a poker game which had established itself with much ingenuity amongst the baggage in front of us, he added, 'and your husband, he is still . . .?'

'Oh yes, he's alive,' I answered quickly, 'he's still in Frankfurt,' and I found myself adding, 'alive – just one of the few.'

I do not know if something in my voice struck a hidden chord, but it was as if a shadow passed across his face. I had been mistaken, it was no longer so young. Handsome, yes, fresh-cheeked, just not so young any more. 'I know what you mean,' he said simply, and then added with a smile which immediately recaptured his youth, 'at least you have three very nice little Krauts to show for it.'

I hesitated a moment, and am not sure if I would have

1 See *The Past is Myself*.

spoken more. It was the sudden change in his expression, his knowing what I meant by being 'still alive' which made me wonder. But the moment, if there had ever been one, was lost – when a cheerful face barely visible behind a huge moustache was thrust round a trap door to the front of the plane which presumably led to the cockpit.

'OK lads, get ready for take-off.' Order was established immediately with military precision. The poker game faded out in seconds, safety straps were adjusted, life-jackets donned and inflated and, as the giant engines sprang to life one after the other with ear-splitting roars, we were all lodged in our places as rigid as robots.

The din did not lessen after the bumps and jolts gave place to pitching and rearing, so that except for an occasional nod and smile, and one fruitless mouthing to the children to go slow on the doughnuts, conversation ceased and I was left with my own wandering thoughts, which I found I could not focus properly yet on an England I had not seen for more than six years. Instead they seemed bent on drifting back to Rohrbach, to my people there, unable to speak French, unable to communicate with their masters, still waiting in hope that their missing menfolk would return. Alois, young Sepp, Friedl, Frau Muckle's Ernst. The second hay-cut would be finished now and the cattle back in their sheds, but soon would come the snows, and the potatoes must be dug from the ground and stored and those giant logs dragged down from the forests. Maybe it was easier to think of the Rohrbach villagers for there was something in the rhythm of their lives which was certain of survival and I had not yet the courage to think too long of those others – Adam, Carl, Helmuth, Claus Stauffenberg – whose dreams and plans had come to nothing, their potential recklessly sacrificed.[1] Lexi who had told me of those meat-hook hangings after 20th July after the plot that failed – where was Lexi now?

Far away, lost in my thoughts, I had barely realized that

1 See *The Past is Myself*.

the shudders, the dives and the jerks of the plane had become noticeably more pronounced, but the door to the cockpit opened once more and the appearance of the cheerful gentleman with the whiskers brought me back from the past. This time he struggled down the length of the cabin, to shout at us in sparkling humour that due to adverse weather conditions we would be unable to land near London, that he was not certain where exactly our 'ditching' would take place, but we were to cheer up as, ha! ha!, he did not expect much flak.

I glanced at the children, who in spite of the racket seemed fast asleep, as were the little German war-bride and her baby. My neighbour, too, his book dropped to the floor, was sleeping. But I could not sleep for whenever I closed my eyes they floated in from the mists, those shadowy faces, faces I loved and had left behind, faces of some still living, faces of others I would never see again.

The dim lights in the cabin snuffed out suddenly, and as the plane plunged on in the darkness, the fleeting images became blurred and faded out, and I, too, must have fallen asleep, only to be woken either by the sudden silencing of the engine roar or by Nicky's anxious thumping on my life-jacket.

'Oh, *Mami*, come on, wake up.' What? – Where? He was pointing to the back of the plane where an open hatchway let in a shaft of light and his voice was shaking with excitement. '*Mami, um Gottes willen!* For God's sake, look!' he said. 'It's England.' I do not know if I had expected Big Ben to be there to greet me, but 'England' turned out to be a deserted airstrip, a few Nissen huts, a smell of the sea and an airforce bus which was to dump us in front of a railway station.

As I clambered out into the pale sunshine and looked about me, I had a strange feeling that I had done all this before. The railway station was unnamed, or rather its name, which I felt should have been proclaimed in bold lettering above the entrance and along the platforms, was covered over with green paint. A tactical measure I had been told, used everywhere in order to mislead the Germans should they decide to land on British soil. There was something else which struck me as unfamiliar about my surroundings in that everything around me seemed so very small. Like Alice in Wonderland, had I grown bigger and bigger? The station which should have been huge and imposing was not very remarkable at all. Now I had it – Westgate-on-Sea, it could try to fox the Germans, but it could not fox me, for when I was a little girl I had spent two not very happy years at boarding-school in this place. Beginning of term, end of term, helpless home-sickness, bubbling excitement; the years had passed, but that little Victorian railway station had not changed, only apparently shrunk.

It had a further trick to play, however, when I approached the ticket-office. 'One single and three halves, please, to London.' 'That'll be ten and six and fifteen bob, twenty-five shillings and sixpence in all' – but I had no money.

'Well then, you and the kids can't travel to London, mum, can you now?' 'Could I telephone?' – Yes, if I had sixpence – but I hadn't sixpence either.

A wary look came over the man's face in the ticket-office, as he turned his attention to the next passenger in the queue. It was his obvious opinion that the lady in front of him was probably not dishonest, but just plain daft.

I was indeed non-plussed, for this was an absurd predicament which I could not have foreseen. 'Operation Woman and Child' – the RAF had fulfilled its duty on landing, and, mission accomplished, was no longer involved.

There was a train standing on the far platform and for a moment I thought of gathering up the luggage, alerting the children and making a dash for it, but I had to discard the idea as being over-ambitious, and was wondering just what I could do when I recognized a welcome voice beside me. It was that of my neighbour on the plane and he was asking me whether I was in trouble and if he could be of any help. Could he help? Oh, certainly he could. He gave me a rather curious look when I took down his name and address in order to repay the five pounds he lent me, but his name, George Millar, did not ring a bell. I heard only later that the boy I had thought too young to be a soldier was a distinguished war-hero, who had been dropped into occupied France dozens of times, contacting the Maquis underground, helping prisoners of war and other dissidents of Hitler's regime to escape across the Channel. He was also one of the few who had survived.

As the train puffed along through the Kent countryside I felt the rising tide of excitement, no different from what it had been years before. Beside me I could hear Nicky patiently teaching Christopher his first words of English. 'Hallo, Granny, I am a little German boy. No, no, not Tsherman, Stophi, J-J-J-Jerman. Now, try again.' Not exactly a very appropriate start I supposed, but never mind, Nicky's accent was still excellent and anyway the clatter of points told me the track was widening – the train was slowing down – we only had another ten minutes to go, I knew it all.

The platform at Victoria Station was crowded with eager, anxious faces expectantly scanning the carriage windows as they passed. A crowd with a difference in that huge moustaches seemed the rage. One particular young man in uniform and similarly equipped seemed to have seen his loved one as he ran along beside our carriage, dodging and smiling and waving his cap. When the train jerked to a stop, to my surprise he flung open the door to our compartment, jumped on board the train, gave me a big kiss and announced happily, 'Well, well, I'm the lucky one,' and then he added, with a laugh, 'don't look so dazed, darling, it's just me, your little brother John.'

It was then his turn to look somewhat taken aback when my elder sons filed out after me and with due respect to his uniform clicked their heels and bowed, and Christopher, not to be outdone, intoned his message of greeting, 'Hallo, Granny, I am a little Tsherman, *nein, nein,* Jerman boy.'

But John took it all in his stride. 'We've all been rushing around from station to station,' he said. 'No one seemed to know where you were landing, but Dad's been alerted and he's on his way from Paddington now.' And even as he spoke I could see another tall figure pushing through the jostling, joyous crowds. Unchanged by the years, it was my father. 'God in heaven, Chriskin,' he said as I rushed forwards and flung my arms around him. 'Dear God, it's wonderful to see you.' And as he held me tightly in a well-remembered hug, I knew that I had come home.

Chapter Three

IN THE YEAR 1945, after the killing ceased, all of Europe's uprooted and scattered peoples seemed to be heading for home. Some for homes no longer to be found under the rubble, others for a haven, an ultimate goal — some promised land in which they could build up their lives all over again.

It was a time when the concept of Home took on almost transcendental qualities — 'There's a long, long trail awinding to the land of my dreams'; 'In der Heimat, der Heimat, da gibt's ein Wiedersehe'n'; 'Dans un coin de mon pays'.

I was one of the privileged few, able to head for home in a country where sixteen miles of water and an island people defending themselves with dogged determination had resulted in most homes remaining intact.

Six long years, and again I was lucky for I found that my father, my mother, my sister and two brothers, all of my close family had survived. Not everything was quite the same: because of the proximity of a military air base and resultant bombs in the grounds, my parents had sold our home near Hatfield and were living in less luxury in Codicote, a Hertfordshire village near Welwyn.

46

My mother only once confessed to a further reason for leaving her home which was that after listening to the thundering overhead as the heavy bombers left for Germany and, mission accomplished, returned again in the early morning, neither she nor my father had been able to sleep all night.

Instead of a flock of retainers, my mother's household now consisted of one faithful and much loved relic of the old days, and two daily ladies who whisked about the place with much enthusiasm, busy in the limited hours at their disposal at what they called 'clearin' up'.

Nor, of course, had we ourselves remained unchanged. My eldest brother Basil, much loved because of his mindfulness as to my well-being when I was doing my first 'season', had married a very beautiful, but somewhat temperamental Russian girl soon after he came down from Cambridge, and it had not been long before they parted company. When war broke out their little son Richard was being cared for by my parents, and my brother, although he should have been dealing in antique furniture for which he had a unique flair, was for some reason or other trying to write a book. Now he was a full-blown colonel, having survived several years of desert warfare in Africa, which I considered some achievement as I could well remember him returning from an OTC (Officers' Training Corps) camp when still at public school, declaring that as far as he could make out the first order to be given to troops if they found themselves in some awkward military situation would be to 'dig latrines'.

My red-headed sister Barbara, whose escapades at boarding-school had not always been much appreciated by a supposedly responsible elder sister, had married a glamorous Australian airman, an Imperial Airways pilot whose base was to become New Zealand. In 1939 she had left with three children and a retinue of nannies and undernannies for the other side of the globe.

When the Japanese entered the war and there were fears of a possible Japanese invasion into New Zealand, her husband, by then an officer in Transport Command, had packed his family into a bomb cradle and flown them to Canada. She had remained there until Transport Command also flew her back to England some weeks before my arrival. She had anticipated the situation by collecting bunk-beds from deserted air-raid shelters and installing them wherever she could find space in my parents' house. As for her tour of the globe, she was heard to declare that as far as she was concerned the inside of a sink looked much the same anywhere in the world.

My younger brother John had been called to the Army when his medical studies were only half-finished. A gay young fellow then, much loved by ladies of all ages, he had been taken prisoner after the landings in Italy and found himself appointed as sole medical officer to a huge POW camp in Germany. It was filled with Polish and Russian prisoners, many of whom should have lived but were doomed to die because suitable medical supplies were either insufficient or non-existent. Doomed to die, sometimes in much pain, because he, the doctor, had no pill or potion with which to keep them alive or ease their going. He was quiet now and rather serious, sometimes staring into the fire as if his thoughts were far away.

My sister's and my children had been little more than toddlers when we left; they were bouncing seven to ten year olds when we returned. The Australian contingent, two girls and a boy, were splendid specimens, equipped with a repertoire of expletives, some of which I had never heard in my life before. This did not deter their German cousins who, although unable to compete, seemed only too willing to learn. An exception was my youngest son, Christopher, aged three, who obviously considered anyone who could not understand the Black Forest dialect to be so dense that they were not worth talking to at all.

Now we were back, and in spite of the initial disappointment at the change in surroundings, I was only too ready to allow the long years of separation to drift away, at least temporarily, into a mist of forgetfulness. I was among my own again, a listener to familiar voices, catching up with a particular family idiom, suddenly overcome by half-remembered smells. Banish the years, I was home, young once more with no responsibilities and there were flowers on the mantelpiece in my bedroom.

The fantasy could not last, for it was not very long before it became clear to my sister and to myself that our mother had nobly bitten off a good deal more than she could chew.

She was a natural home-maker, firmly believing that a home did not consist of merely a roof and four walls, but also of what she called 'those extra bits and pieces' which was her uncomplicated way of describing a certain ambience, a safe and changeless rhythm, generated by both of my parents, which had helped us to grow up and face what was to come, from a background of total security. But although my father, who did not have to suffer it all day, seemed to enjoy the hubbub, I doubt if she had ever dreamed of her orderly home being turned into a multilingual beargarden.

In fact she was already beginning to talk about having to build another house when my sister and I realized that we must stir ourselves and do something about it instead of sitting around talking our heads off over endless cups of tea.

We must learn to accept that not only home conditions, but that England, too, had changed. In Germany I had become accustomed to trying to get around every rule in the book. In post-war England everyone seemed so law-abiding, so virtuous. In Berlin, queue-busting had been one of my favourite pastimes. It was quite a simple game which could start perhaps with a box of fresh spinach or anything unusual in front of a foodstore. Such a delicacy hardly needed to be put on display before a queue of determined *Hausfrauen* seemed to erupt out of the ground and start automatically on the slow shuffle towards a chancy meal. When the shopkeeper's supplies were diminishing by the minute, it was time for the game to start with a discreet murmur to the lady ahead of or behind me: 'Do you remember last week trying to get near those carrots – and we'd hardly arrived up at the front when that black Mercedes rolled up and the chauffeur got out and swiped the lot – I wonder where they went?' If the response to this opening gambit was positive – the neighbour in front or behind murmured back, 'I don't wonder, I know' or perhaps, *'Unerhört'* or, with luck, even, *'Schweinerei'* – my morning was made, for I knew that, with a little encouragement, the solos could become a chorus, shopping bags potential weapons. A horde of steely-eyed housewives were ready to go on the rampage and should a glittering Mercedes dare to draw up anywhere near the foodstore, the driver in his black uniform would be lucky to get away with his life. Meanwhile, she who started the rumpus could stroll forward and collect whatever it was she had been queueing for.

In England there was so much to learn – or unlearn. No black market; no scrounging for that little bit extra on the ration card; queues, however long, must be treated with respect. It started at the bus-stop, where instead of the frantic pushing and shoving in order to get on board that I was used to, civilized behaviour meant waiting in a queue. Wait, now wait, until the conductor's bugle call sounded 'Full up', to put you dutifully back again in your place on the pavement.

It was when standing immobile in such an orderly procession, with my feet getting colder by the minute, that I found myself trying to make out just what had happened to my country. England had won the war, the boys were coming home again, the bells should be ringing out, everything should be so joyous, and yet it was so very dull. I could only come to the conclusion that maybe the effort had been so great that now everyone was simply tired out.

With Christmas around the corner, the newspapers excelled themselves predicting one catastrophe after another waiting to engulf us. The coming winter was to be the coldest in living memory; an influenza epidemic of dire proportions was also on its way; due to a state of near-starvation in Germany, the rations in England could not be kept at the same level for much longer.

There was no official way of communicating with Germany until the victorious powers made up their minds about a Peace Treaty. I knew that cigarettes were hard currency in the Fatherland, so that all I could do about 'near-starvation' was to beg anyone in uniform who happened to be travelling that way to take with them as many cigarettes as they could stuff into their duffel bags and give them to Peter. The lack of any message in return seemed to indicate that they had not arrived at their proper destination.

The day arrived when my mother and I were seated alone at the breakfast table dissecting a pat of butter into minute portions destined to last the family for the day. I knew that we were both thinking about my sister. She was with us yesterday, why not today? The opening door gave us the answer as she stood there shivering and shaking, her cheeks about the colour of her hair. The 'flu epidemic we had been warned about had arrived on our doorstep a week earlier, and now it was only for the coldest winter in living memory to follow suit in order to complete the newspapers' predictions.

'It's a sort of ten green bottles situation – then there were only two,' remarked my mother rather wearily as she packed my sister off to bed to join the rest of the household in awaiting the arrival of an over-worked doctor whose sole prescription consisted of bustling from patient to patient telling them in breezy tones to 'Cheer up'.

Left on my own at the breakfast table I found myself staring disconsolately at the tiny blobs of butter lined up in front of me and I knew that my usually fairly dependable spirits were sinking so fast that it could not be long before they reached rock bottom.

So this was the home that I had dreamed about. No matter how often I reminded myself that I was privileged and surely ungrateful, it had to be faced that I had wasted a great deal of time longing for something which could never return. It was nobody's fault but my own that I could not adjust to a new situation. I was a survivor, oh yes, but I was branded by Hitler, by war, by failure, almost by the fact that I had not ended in a gas chamber. To add to my troubles I was very likely to get the 'flu.

If you have been given an almighty fright make a rush for the nearest lavatory; when in trouble go for a brisk walk.

Two oft-repeated axioms learned in the nursery flashed across my mind and I decided to leave the family rations to look after themselves — they could melt if they felt like it — but I would head for the garden.

I pushed back the curtains, opened the french windows and stepped out, to be greeted by a blast of ice-cold air which nearly took my breath away. The lawn was no longer green and welcoming as it had been yesterday, but stretched out before me, cold, rigid and white as a deserted ice-rink. Not to be deterred I stomped over to the low wall which overlooked the main road to the village where muffled figures in army greatcoats were busy removing the remains of some lumps of concrete. These, I had been told, were intended to protect Codicote from an invasion of German tanks; the war, including its absurdities, was still with us. Back then past a bed of dahlias, ablaze with colour yesterday, but which had suffered an overnight defeat, and were now jet black. Some roses seemed to have survived the sudden winter onslaught, but this was not surprising seeing that they had also managed to out-live the mis-kicked footballs of our children.

By the time I passed through the vegetable garden and arrived at the plot where my parents, determined not to go under, had decided to build a small house for my sister, I realized that this relatively straightforward cure for low spirits was beginning to make itself felt. After all, things were not altogether hopeless. In our efforts to lessen the burden on our parents, my sister and I had decided that our boys at least must go to boarding-school. We had found one in Pyrford where the headmaster, a Mr Pooley, faced the prospect of trying to educate two little Germans and one Aussie with complete equanimity, assuring us that he found the prospect not only interesting, but exciting. He would have no difficulty with Nicky, who was British born and since his arrival had slipped into the scene as if he had always belonged.

I was not so sure about my middle son, John, as he still referred to Berlin as home and when his English was challenged or laughed at was inclined to reply with his fists.

As for Christopher, a sturdy three year old, we could perhaps persuade Madi, a former governess, to take charge.

Briskly now, Chris, briskly. Once more round the garden and by the time I was back near the house I was practically running, glowing all over from the crisp cold air and a newly discovered sense of purpose.

Up the stairs with the breakfast trays, and it was almost as if several nebulous hopes and half-cooked plans were already on the road to possible achievement.

Gently, now gently, one thing at a time. Firstly, I decided that I must do something about regaining my British nationality. I was fed up with being German, and the law of the land now allowed me to do so. Then, I would try to communicate with someone whom I had not seen since before the war when Adam brought him to our house in Berlin and described him when we met for the last time, as possibly the only real friend he had left in England: David Astor, a son of Nancy Astor whose parliamentary forays, according to an uncle of mine, were guaranteed to liven up the place. I could remember David as tall, fair haired and boyish looking, whose shy almost diffident manner belied not only a shrewd knowledge of the political scene, but an instinctive understanding of the situation in which we found ourselves. It was July 1939 and his visit had done us all good, lifting for a while a sense of helplessness and isolation, as Hitler's war crept up on us, nearer and nearer, day by day. I had reason to believe that Adam had made contact with him during the war; as I galloped up and down the stairs with those breakfast trays I made up my mind to do likewise.

A telephone call, and two days later the Green Line bus rattled me off to London and deposited me back in Codicote in the evening. The hours between passed quickly for Adam's friend had hardly changed, except that he had since married and was now Foreign Editor of the *Observer*. The same boyish good looks. The same shy, almost self-effacing, manner, but, above all, when it came to problems, I was to meet with a unique sense of personal involvement and an immediate

53

searching for some solution. I could well understand why Adam considered him to be someone very special.

I considered that I had plenty of problems. How was I to relieve my parents' household? Get back to Germany even temporarily? In moments when I felt extra privileged, I had even wondered about trying to do something for the widows and children of the 20th July Plot, some of whom were in dire straits. But what was the use? How could one launch into such things? David Astor seemed to take all such matters in his stride. I must of course first regain my British citizenship, after which he managed to persuade me with infinite tact that his newspaper was in dire need of a correspondent with knowledge of the German scene who could also speak the language fluently. He was even willing to tackle the problem of helping the 20th July widows, which he considered to be a splendid idea. The British were compulsively generous; they just did not know that there had been a Germany other than Hitler's. Such a venture could become a bridge, bringing English women, possibly also war widows, together with Germans who were likewise having to face up to life alone. It must be a Trust Fund with charitable status. Victor Gollancz, who had founded the charity 'Save Europe Now', would be the man to give us advice as to the setting up of such a Trust. We must have a Patron, and Lady Cripps, wife of Sir Stafford who was now Chancellor of the Exchequer, would be the ideal person. Both she and Sir Stafford had known and always trusted Adam during the war, and a letter to *The Times* signed by her would be just right to get things started. He knew of another girl, Diana Hopkinson, who would be only too willing to help. An address? We could use the *Observer*.

I had little to offer in return beyond giving him as clear a picture as possible of the life we had led since our last meeting, and as the daylight faded and the London lights came to life (not quite as brightly as in days gone by), he listened to me in complete silence, not stirring, just glancing at me now and again with an expression on his face as if he were having to go through some of these things himself.

As I lay in bed that night random thoughts passed through my mind, one almost making me want to laugh aloud. As an Official Correspondent for the *Observer* in Germany, I would have to wear a uniform; my brother John had already offered to lend me his battle jacket. Non-fraternization was the order of the day in Germany though and it was strictly forbidden even to smile at a German, let alone embrace one. What in God's name would be Peter's reaction at having to meet up again with his lawfully wedded wife dressed up in such singular fashion? But I had relearned today that problems were there to be overcome, no more useless moaning, no more uncertainty. I was back on course again and I turned on my side and was soon fast asleep.

Chapter Four

THE PLANE WHICH transported me back to the Fatherland some weeks later was much the same as that which I had boarded with the children many months previously. Transport Command, no comforts provided, everyone in uniform, including myself. Our destination was Hamburg and I had been careful to pack an extra supply of cigarettes in my duffel bag in the hope of dumping them with Peter's mother who lived in Aumühle. To judge from the shape of the boxes and bundles strewn about by my fellow passengers, their contents were not dissimilar. I was a little unsure about my get-up, except for my beret with its golden 'C' badge on a green ground which I thought rather smart. The rest of my rig-out was borrowed, and at the last minute my elder brother, who had never felt warm since leaving the desert, had insisted on my taking along his army greatcoat which was far too big and troubled me with the thought that the whole ensemble made me look rather like Hermann Goering. But on this, my first journey back to Germany, I had a good deal more to think about than my appearance.

True, after my first bus trip to London when David Astor had picked up the pieces of my shattered morale and launched me on this unusual expedition, I could be glad that things on the home front seemed to be sorting themselves out. Perhaps the elements had something to do with it, for, as if trying to compensate for the atrocious weather served up during the winter, spring had burst upon us quite suddenly; an English spring bringing with it all the warmth, life and colour which I had so often dreamed might come my way again one day.

As the weather picked up the congestion in my parents' house and the temper of its occupants improved likewise. It had not taken too long before my elder boys, who had been going to the local day school, were able to speak quite passable English and, with the language barrier behind them, they were teaming up and becoming good friends with their cousins. They all now had bicycles provided by my long-suffering but also cunning parents and seemed willing to sacrifice their foot-balls and depart on long trips around the countryside. They had also set up a putting green on the lawn which gave my father much pleasure as he was a superb golfer and, far from flailing each other with golf clubs, they, particularly Nicky, seemed eager to learn the game.

My indefatigable mother, in spite of her moral principles, had managed to bypass building regulations and obtain permission to build what she called an 'experimental house'. Nobody knew exactly what was to be experimental about it, but before I left, the foundations were already laid and there was plenty of activity going on at the far end of the vegetable garden.

My sister's and my plan to send our school-age sons to boarding-school had also worked out well, and a fortnight before my departure, they, too, had left for Dane Court, a prep school in Surrey, wielding their brand-new tuck-boxes and looking surprisingly British after exchanging their leather pants for grey flannel suits and round, rusty-red school caps. A subsequent telephone call had assured me that they were 'settling well', whatever that might mean, but I could also gather from their accounts that the atmosphere in the school was such that they had met up with no national prejudice whatsoever. That left only Christopher – and here I had been lucky too when I managed to persuade our former governess Madi to come along, at least temporarily, in order to keep an eye on him. In my young days she had been supposed to teach us French but, as she came from the Alsace, she also spoke some German and, since she had never put the wind up any of us, I had to hope that all would go well.

I had applied to become British once again and although I had no passport yet, the fact that I could travel in uniform on a Control Commission pass seemed to indicate that I had already been welcomed back to the fold.

So far so good, but ever since I had accepted the *Observer*'s original offer with alacrity, a small, but increasing cloud was looming on the horizon. I had been fairly confident that my successful arrangement with Madi would survive even if I were not always there to give her a hand. But I had forgotten that in the meantime Madi, too, had grown older and was much less mobile, and even on my short trips to London I could sense my now four-year-old son had got her measure. Warning bells sounded ominously whenever I returned, giving me to understand that much though she loved us, it would not be long before she would find herself forced to depart from sheer exhaustion.

At David Astor's suggestion I turned up as frequently as I could at the *Observer*'s offices in Tudor Street in order to get some idea as to how a newspaper functioned. I always tried to be there on Thursdays, as that was the day when they held their weekly editorial conference. This rather splendid title proved to be a congenial get-together presided over by the editor, Ivor Brown. It took place in a small dimly lit room around a long narrow table smothered with an assortment of books and papers.

The editor himself appeared to me at first to be a pillar of silence who, should he decide to interrupt the general chatter at all, would merely ask rather gruffly such questions as, 'Well now, what about Spain?' or, 'All right, let us turn to Africa'. As a raw recruit, I sometimes found myself wondering how on earth any newspaper, let alone one so prestigious, could possibly appear in thousands three days later. It needed quite a few such sessions before I realized how privileged I was to be among a team of young journalists who were already well on their way to becoming stars in their profession.

After a cup of rather wishy-washy tea which usually terminated the proceedings, I only had to climb a few flights of stairs in order to take part in a hive of activity of a different nature: the 20th July Memorial Fund which, like many another charity perhaps, had come to life by way of random thought; ours had been simply to try to find a way of diffusing the post-war atmosphere of hatred and mistrust which existed between Britain and Germany. We hoped to cross a divide by bringing English families together with German counterparts who had been widowed or orphaned after the failure of the 1944 Bomb Plot to rid the world of Hitler. When Lady Cripps and the Bishop of Chichester agreed to become our patrons, and an appeal signed by them had been launched in *The Times* as well as the *Observer*, the response had been overwhelming. So here in an even smaller room which looked out towards the dome of St Paul's, I could find Diana Hopkinson battling with a typewriter she had not made use of since she was an Oxford student, and also Gritta Weill who had been seconded by the *Observer* to give us much needed help with the flood of letters and parcels which were arriving daily on the newspaper's doorstep.

There is something nice and exhilarating in doing what my mother would have called 'good works', so that, perched high above the city roof-tops, we certainly enjoyed ourselves trying to cope with the unexpected avalanche of good will. Even the return trip to Codicote no longer seemed so cheerless for, after reading some of the letters and sorting through the parcels, I was convinced that beneath the humdrum, clothes-coupon-clad exteriors of at least some of my fellow travellers, there must surely beat hearts of gold.

It was after one Thursday session that David told me that news had reached him which might mean my leaving for Germany as soon as possible. Political life there was seemingly beginning to stir, with some Germans already trying to start up new political parties, and he was thinking of having more permanent representation over there. Post-Nazi Germany was still practically an unknown political territory and as I could speak the language and knew the country so well I could surely be of help in providing reliable and trustworthy contacts. He was also concerned about Adam von Trott's family since, because of the postal censorship, he had had no news from them for some time.

So it was that in May 1946, all dressed up in khaki, I was airborne making my way towards Hamburg. In spite of the roar of the plane's engines, and my real joy at the thought of seeing Peter again, the sound ringing in my ears was Christopher's cry of, 'Back soo, Mami, *bitte, bitte*, back soo' as he was led away by gentle enough guardians who in my eyes had suddenly become determined wardresses.

A message had been sent off to Peter telling him of my possible arrival, but I had no idea as to whether or not he had received it. It so happened that he had done and, with faithful Freda in tow, had managed to scrounge an old Volkswagen, and they had driven from Frankfurt since dawn in order to be in Hamburg on time.

The shock when we did meet was not too shattering as, not knowing of my outward transformation, he failed to pick me out of the khaki torrent which poured off the plane, and was about to leave the airstrip when Freda, not easily thwarted, spotted my pseudo-military presence, rushed up and flung her arms around me, greatcoat and all. Chatting away nineteen to the dozen, she danced along ahead of me towards the retreating figure of my unsuspecting husband and when we caught up with him we all simply burst out laughing.

We had not left all complications behind us however, as Peter, who had been up since dawn, was beginning to feel the strain of dodging behind giant military transport in a Beetle which had seen better days, and it seemed that both he and Freda had to be off the road by curfew time. So we decided that we would have to find some place to stay the night.

We had not yet quite realized the implications of our situation, so it was a bit disconcerting when we stopped before the entrance to an estate somewhere near Hanover which had obviously been requisitioned by the Allies. After much telephoning back and forth, the sentry at the gates informed us that I would be welcome to spend the night in the castle itself, whereas my 'chauffeur' and my 'secretary' could only be accommodated in the sergeants' quarters which were situated somewhere in the stables.

My first night back in Germany therefore was spent in much luxury. Shades of my 'deb' days! Here was I toasting the King and chatting with fresh-faced, glossy-haired boys who, in spite of their immaculate uniforms, seemed equally overwhelmed by the elevated circumstances in which they found themselves.

Peter and Freda for their part enjoyed a far livelier evening, being fed to bursting with sausages and scrambled eggs, washed down with strong sweet tea known as 'army brew' and later, after Freda had wisely retired to her quarters, with gallons of good strong ale. Such were the festivities that the following morning Peter could only remember rollicking out songs which repeatedly referred to some place called Blighty, and a final decision arrived at by one and all that it would not be long before they would all be marching together against the Russians.

On the following day we set off for Frankfurt and as our route brought us near to Imshausen, Adam von Trott's family home, we decided to make a slight detour and look in on Adam's widow, Clarita. It was a joy to find her reunited once more with her two little girls and also doing her best to come to terms with life without him.

After the failure of the 20th July Bomb Plot, Clarita had been imprisoned and the children removed from the care of their grandmother, given false names and transported to a camp for children on the North Sea coast. Rumour had it that Hitler had demanded that the offspring of such 'traitors' should also be wiped out. But there must have been some remnants of humanity left in a few of his underlings because the order was never carried out, and luckily for the little von Trotts, the sister-in-charge had carefully noted down all the real names of the children in her care. So shortly after hostilities ended, Elsa and Ilse could become Verena and little Clarita once again. Indeed, a few days before our visit, one of the guards who had fetched them away had returned to Imshausen to apologize for his deed. Adam's mother was a majestic figure and he confessed that he could not forget the look of utter contempt that had come over her face at the time, and her telling him that she had not thought that she would ever have to admit to feeling shame at being a German.

In Frankfurt I found myself billeted in the Press Camp which had been a former hotel and was near the main railway station. It was an important part of the city because it housed the black market which had become one of the busiest in post-war Europe. I had known of its existence before, but now it was just around the corner and from my window I could watch GIs by the dozen bargaining with the native Germans, mostly women, who turned up every day with their wares – jewellery, cameras, watches. If necessary, they included themselves in the deal in order to stock up with coffee, sugar, alcohol and, above all, cigarettes. Every so often an army jeep manned by military police would patrol noisily up and down the street and the crowd disappeared into doors and alleyways, only to reappear as soon as the crisis had passed.

I had found it difficult to conform to the orderliness of law-abiding post-war England, but now I was being confronted with another side to the picture, and could see for myself that when certain circumstances prevail, civilized behaviour can easily be cast to the winds.

In the Press Camp I could listen to an otherwise congenial fellow, willing to treat the Germans fairly, eager to show them what democracy was all about. But then there was the problem of that out-size cuckoo clock he'd found hanging on the wall of the flat allotted to him. His kids would go wild about it, but Uncle Sam would have to provide him with a crate to ship it home when he next went on leave to the States. He was not the only one to have problems, for according to allied directives non-fraternization was still in force. Peter could therefore not cross the threshold of the Press Camp which was off-limits to civilians while I, being part of the Allied Forces set-up, could not go home without an official permit to do so. Peter still lived in our little house in Kronberg looked after by Freda, as were other homeless refugees. She herself was awaiting the release of her husband, Hannes, who, although he had been one of the noisiest of our anti-Nazi friends, had been arrested by the Allies because of his rank in the Ministry of the Interior.

There are certain situations so absurd that no rule or regulation, however strictly enforced, can hope to be obeyed. It is then, I guess, that human judgement must come to the rescue. In our case humanity triumphed when Pat Nicholson, Dick O'Regan and Betty entered our lives.

Dick was a restless go-ahead young journalist working for Associated Press, willing to jump a train, hitch a ride, barge in anywhere to pick up a good story. It was therefore heart-warming to see how much time he spent 'interviewing' Peter at just about lunchtime in the Press Camp or in the evenings when the bar was crowded and multi-coloured, lethal-looking concoctions were doing the rounds. Betty was working freelance, although instinct told me it would not be long before she became Mrs O'Regan. Pat Nicholson was a lovely looking girl, whose dazzling white teeth and slim legs stamped her unmistakably as 'Made In America'. She held the rank of captain and a key position in the administration of the Press Camp, for she ruled over the office which dispensed passes in and out of the premises and could thus control where anyone happened to be at any given time.

'Gee, Chris, why that's a real laugh!' she remarked after hearing my unusual tale and, although otherwise scrupulous about her work, she proceeded to hand me out a travel permit whenever I needed one to wherever I wished to go; she also managed to provide transport whenever she had a jeep to spare.

From then on both Peter and I, motorized as often as not

and armed with necessary travel permits, could move around as we wished, and naturally I headed immediately for our little house in Kronberg, where some of my civilian clothes were still hanging in the cupboard.

In Kronberg the house itself appeared to have become more like a transit camp than a home. Except for Peter and Freda whose bedrooms actually contained beds, further furnishings in passageways and the attic seemed to consist of a jumble of mattresses and sleeping-bags, the odd chair and a lamp. The kitchen downstairs was the centre of a household where Freda, an enthusiastic but atrocious cook, spent much time dishing out curious messes which I could now augment with tins of US army rations. Thank goodness my love for Freda did not depend on her cooking. 'People come and go you see, Chris, it's a roof and sometimes even quite warm and they don't mind a bit what they get to eat,' she would announce cheerfully, although even she had to admit that once, having boiled up some old fish bones and presented the result as *Bouillabaisse à la Rechenberg*, Peter had tried one spoonful and emptied the rest out of the window. 'So you see, your old pan with the somersaults came in useful after all!' she concluded with supreme lack of concern.

The only addition to the household and now part of the kitchen equipment was a rusty old sewing-machine which she told me she had picked up outside one of the requisitioned villas up the road. It had certainly seen better days and took up a lot of room, but I could not help feeling glad of it because it signified that in spite of our dire predictions, Freda had not given up her venture into dressmaking.

Chapter Five

MY FIRST ASSIGNMENT as a War Correspondent, if I can call it that, was intended to last some three to four weeks, after which I was due back in England for the boys' summer holidays. It did not take long before I began to feel extremely uncomfortable in my phoney role.

I was conscious that my main reason for coming back to Germany had been to see Peter, to discover how he was faring and, if possible, to plan with him some future for ourselves and our family. I could not type and had no idea how to manipulate the stops and wires which carried any useful piece of information back to the newspaper. True, unlike most other representatives of my adopted profession who had to pick up their material from informants able to speak their language, I could speak fluent German, and had some experience of the twelve years which had gone before. This should have been an asset; I did not find it so.

In fact as I travelled between the comparative comfort of the 'Ami Ghetto' and the under-privileged world outside, I found myself becoming increasingly confused and angry, and was probably not being fair to anyone.

On the one side were my American cousins, glowing with

health, touchingly friendly, possibly lonely, but happy enough it would seem, so long as the *Fräuleins* were willing and the plumbing functioned smoothly wherever they were billeted. If they thought at all of the role they had been forced to play in reconstructing a new and democratic Germany, they had a further national obsession to call upon – 'classification'. How could you recognize a Nazi if you saw one? How to separate the wolves from the lambs? Quite simple really, Uncle Sam had the answer, classify the lot and proceed from there—

On the other side were the left-overs of the defeated Master Race, drowning in self-pity, for whom a sympathetic ear in allied uniform was a chance not to be missed. I did not know Frankfurt well as a town, except that it had been the centre of Germany's huge chemical and leather industries, and having to watch the dismantling of their mighty empires must have been hard for some of its citizens to take. All the same, the ceaseless wailing coming from those whose finances might now be in the doldrums, but who had otherwise lived comfortably through the Nazi years, could succeed in bringing me to a point of near explosion.

'We who have so suffered, Frau Bielenberg, and are suffering now.' Suffered – suffering? My hat!!

Boys dying on far-flung battlefields had suffered – suffered in the desert and in the snows, and some were still suffering in Russian POW camps. What about the posters plastering the walls, the films from the concentration camps, the piles of starved skeletons, the gas chambers? This was no longer rumour, this was fact. To blazes with their complaints and their suffering! As far as I was concerned they could all take up their worthless share portfolios and go jump in the Rhine.

It soon became clear to me that, being not only under-privileged but constantly under their orders professionally, Peter had become almost hostile to the Allies. It just did not suit him to be an underdog and, in order to remain happy together, we decided that the allied occupation of his country should, if possible, remain a closed subject between us.

Our pact was not always easy to abide by, for clouds of

66

misunderstanding threatened it from all sides. We managed fairly successfully until I was approached one evening in Kronberg by a gentleman whom I had seen there once before and not much liked. After drawing me aside he told me in a conspiratorial whisper that he had information to give me from an absolutely impeccable source which he felt I should know about.

It appeared that the British, instead of trying to feed their zone of occupation to the best of their ability, were allowing planeloads of food, particularly butter, to take off from Hamburg every day bound for London. Was he certain of his source? Indeed he was and if necessary could supply me with the times of their departure. I was deeply shocked, hardly able to believe that behind a smoke-screen of morality the British were behaving much like the French, who were systematically clearing their zone of wine and timber and anything else that they could profitably lay their hands on. The thought of those minute pats of butter at home flashed across my mind, but at least they turned up every morning, whereas I knew that even in the American zone many had not seen butter for months.

It was not easy to penetrate the security network with which the higher-ups in Military government surrounded themselves and the badge on my cap which betrayed my connection with Press and publicity was not helpful. So when I finally manoeuvred my way to my desired goal I was glad to meet a personable young officer who welcomed me to share his pot of tea. After the usual opening remarks about the weather, I asked him if he would perhaps tell me whether transport planes loaded with food were taking off from Hamburg or Bremen airfields every day. 'Oh yes, indeed they are,' came his prompt reply. 'Every day for the last fortnight,' – and their destination? Well, Berlin of course, had I not heard that conditions in the British Sector were far worse than in the American zone? 'We may have to step it up next week if I can get the Yanks to give us a hand with more supplies,' he added, obviously unable to fathom the look of profound relief which must have come over my face.

The sense of relief soon vanished; instead, long before I got back to Frankfurt, I was ready to explode.

I do not lose my temper very often but when I do I gather that it is better to keep out of my way, and allow me to bawl my head off for a while until I peter out. Only a year back this particular characteristic had come to my rescue just before my interrogation in Gestapo Headquarters when I'd been forced to witness a Gestapo woman slapping the face of an elderly prisoner sitting before her in chains. After that I had been scared no longer, but was able to bounce into my interrogation, borne on wings of rage.

Freda was cranking away at her ancient sewing-machine when I burst into the kitchen the following day. I was still on the rampage. 'Listen, Fredachen,' I announced in clarion tones, 'you may or may not have heard of the latest wild goose chase that stinker sent me on, but all I can say is I'm simply fed up. I've got to the stage of wishing I hadn't come, and I'm glad I'm going. OK, I can see from your face that you don't like him either—then why does he come here? Why does Peter have such bloody liars about the place? Why do I have to meet them and listen to their dreary complaints? Has he forgotten how it used to be? How can he surround himself with such second-raters? To listen to them you'd think the Americans had started the whole business. I can assure you they don't want to be here either. They'd be far happier rocking on some porch in Ohio or some other damn place. Butter to London, for God's sake! Types like him would have been informers in the old days, ready to carry their snivelling little bits of information to the Gestapo.'

I sensed I was being unreasonable and probably also beginning to simmer down for I found myself adding more quietly, 'The real trouble is, Fredachen, Peter and I are drifting apart. I don't really understand anything any more. I know it's terrible to say so, but sometimes I don't care if I never see Germany again.'

Freda's machine had stopped its rhythmic clanking and she was sitting back, looking at me with eyes as clear blue as an autumn sky. She was also shaking her head as if she did not want to hear. 'Now, now, Chris,' she said. 'Take off your cap and sit down – that's better. Well now, let me do the talking for a bit. You've been here exactly a fortnight, and we were all just so happy to see you back but don't forget, Peter has been here for months without you, and although I know you both decided not to talk about what has been going on here in the meantime, I'm not so sure that it was such a wise thing to do after all.

'You see, Peter had to get a job of some kind and with his clean political record and his knowledge of English that was easy enough. I'm not sure whether he was already with the *Metallgesellschaft* before you left, but, if you remember, when I arrived on the scene he'd already been given the task of helping the Americans in what they were calling "de-Nazification". I know he took it on in good faith – you see, I think he feels as I do that anyone who has survived has a duty to do what they can – but I guess it was not long after you left before he wished he hadn't. I don't know if you have looked at the huge *Fragebogen* which has been doing the rounds since Christmas, well I have. It's a questionnaire which has to be filled out by everyone in the zone so that Military government can decide who has been a Nazi and who not.

'According to the answers received, the plan is then to divide the population into five categories from major offenders, lesser offenders down to those who can be exonerated. Then the baddies will be punished, the goodies let off and that's that. It all sounds quite dotty to me – almost like trying to psychoanalyse a whole nation. Surely, Chrislein, you and I would have lost our touch if we couldn't spot a real Nazi if we met one, but no, they want it all in black and white. Listen to this one about religion. "With what church are you affiliated? Have you ever severed your connection with any church officially or unofficially? If so, give particulars and reasons?" Oh dear, I remember that one because Furtwängler's Berlin housekeeper turned up here the other day and asked me to give her a hand with the questions as she couldn't make head or tail of most of them. She knew the answer to this one though and told me to write down, "I stopped going to church when an Allied bomb hit it and killed the parson". As you see, *Berlin bleibt Berlin*!

'But back to your poor Peter, he's in the middle of it, although he only has to deal with industrialists who either want to hang on to their businesses or start up new ones and can't do so unless they can prove a non-Nazi past. Let me tell you, dear, these are not friends about the place as we had in the old days – they died, Chris, they died, or are scattered to the winds. These I suppose could be called new acquaintances, most of them wanting Peter's help to start their lives over again and so long as they have a legitimate case he is willing to do so.

'One other thing which I only learned lately was that when the Americans occupied Italy they enrolled a whole lot of expatriate Italians into their administration and the result was fine. They could speak the language, they were glad to be back there and when it came to fiddling and diddling no one knew better than they how to cope with their former countrymen. So it soon became a very happy, not over-pedantic family set-up which functioned very well.

'I think they hoped to repeat the performance here in Germany with German expatriates but these were of course, unfortunately, mainly Jews. Well, you can't expect Jews to love us, Chris, and I guess you can't blame them if they throw their weight around. But the fact remains, most of them refuse to speak German and their English is as bad as my cooking. They expect Germans to stand to attention when spoken to, and they don't believe a word they say anyway.

'So think of your Peter, eager to get things right, who has never exactly been a paragon when it comes to patience, or for that matter being subordinate. Why he never even stood up when his interrogator came into his cell in Ravensbrück! "Stand up for that bastard, I just couldn't." Do you remember?

'I don't know if he told you about the incident the other day when he brought a case to whichever official was in charge of such things in Military government. I know he'd prepared it most carefully, all about some fellow who had joined the SS in the hope of protecting his half-Jewish wife and of keeping his brother-in-law's firm intact. He'd done nothing culpable and had succeeded in protecting his wife and her brother, but according to the *Fragebogen* the SS ticket was enough to deprive him of his livelihood and send him to jail.

'Anyway, this particular official listened to him in silence and said nothing even when he'd finished. So Peter suggested that if he couldn't understand English perhaps they'd better speak German. He told me he'd spoken very politely but somehow I doubt it. Anyway at that the officer jumped to his feet and yelled "*Raus* – get out" – flung him out in fact, although I can't think he could have done much flinging as according to Peter he was small and round and looked as if he'd never worn a uniform in his life before. Peter left, but I'm afraid one of these days if something similar happens again he won't, he'll simply knock one of them over the head with his briefcase, and land himself in another detention camp – but an American one this time.

'So listen, dear, if you want my advice, here it is. Get him out, persuade him to get out if you can – and soonest.

'Just one last thing before I shut up. I think you should realize that there are plenty of love-sick females about the place just now and, except for the Americans, very few men. As you've doubtless noticed, Peter is very good looking, and if you are not around he's also, so to speak, available. I love you both but you can't expect me to remain a watchdog forever.'

Freda had risen to her feet before delivering her ultimatum and was eyeing me sternly. But, even as she spoke, her expression changed from that of a miniature recording angel to one of amazement. I watched too, as, slowly yet purposefully, a strange multi-coloured excrescence seemed to be pushing its way out from the innards of her rusty sewing-machine.

'It looks like a lump of squished cotton or something,' I said. 'We'll have to poke about a bit.'

But Freda was not listening. Instead she was banging

71

the table and shouting quite as loudly as ever I had, 'Damn, damn, damn, damn! – damn this rotten machine – damn the Germans – damn the Allies – damn the war, damn, well, damn everything!!' Whereupon she sat down suddenly and burst into tears.

'OK, Freda – you win – I'll be back again after the holidays and I'll try my best to get that exit permit for Peter even if it's only a temporary one – my father's already doing all he can. I'm sure there are others who'll give me a hand.'

I was trying with no success to be of some comfort until finally all I could find to say was, 'Oh, do stop crying, or I'll start off too.'

So we mopped ourselves up with one of my brother's khaki handkerchiefs and jabbed away together at that ridiculous lump of cotton until it gave in. A minor mystery was solved when Freda remarked casually that the eruption might have had something to do with the scrapings off the frying-pan which, due to a lack of oil, she had emptied into the contraption that morning. I defy anyone to remain in the dumps after that piece of information, and so it was not long before harmony was restored. As a result of our combined efforts the cogs and wheels were functioning as smoothly as could ever be hoped for and we could rest assured that with luck the fashion world need have no fears that Maison Rechenberg's unique collection might suddenly go off the market.

Chapter Six

ONE JOURNEY WHICH I knew I must make before leaving for England was to travel back to Rohrbach, even if I might feel rather foolish doing so in khaki regalia at the wheel of an American jeep. There was something about that small corner of Germany which I hoped might help to wipe away the artificial world I seemed to be living in and carry me back to simple sanity.

I wished I could have had Peter with me, but there was something about the French occupied zone which he found uncomfortable. He was unable to communicate, and although he knew well how the Germans had behaved in France, it was not easy to experience revenge.

In the French zone little towns such as Furtwangen were still overladen with tricolours, but *Spahis* and *goumiers* no longer roamed the streets, having been replaced by hordes of French civilians. This had come about because, as soon as the combat troops departed and the regular occupation forces took their place, they had been allowed to import their families; their wives, their children, their mothers, grandmothers, aunts, uncles, nephews, nieces – the lot. This pragmatic arrangement had possibly helped to solve the problems of food and housing shortages in France, but added an extra burden on those who were trying to live and make ends meet in occupied Germany.

Nonetheless I found the attitude of the Germans towards their conquerors healthier than in the other zones since they were not being asked to show a respect which they certainly did not feel. On the whole they seemed to take the view that 'we gave it to them, now they are giving it to us and no moral implications need be involved'.

Rohrbach itself had not changed at all, and except for the white table-cloth spread out in my honour over the Mayor's *Stammtisch* (special table) and the wine glasses usually produced for weddings and funerals, the *Gaststube* in the Adler, which soon filled to overflowing, received me as one of its own again.

We had plenty to talk about although I had to re-accustom myself to the dialect in order to learn what had been going on in the valley since my departure. Sepp, in fulfilment of his prophecy as to his post-war activities made to me during the war, still mended shoes and manned the telephone which he hoped might recover one day from the treatment it had received at the hands of the *Ingénieurs*.

The Mayor, whose re-election in spite of our intervention with the *Gouverneur* in Villingen had suffered a temporary set-back, had been forced into temporary retirement. But this was a problem soon solved by the villagers themselves who, by interpreting the newly established democratic process in their own way, soon had him back again at the head of their community.

Only Frau Muckle gave me cause for concern for she had aged considerably and lost weight, and her rheumatism seemed to plague her more than I could remember. Filled with hope, she still kept my cardboard Union Jack stuck up in the window, but after our departure this had not saved the Adler from being overrun with French troops. Some had behaved as soldiers sometimes do, spreading their bulky equipment all over the place, eating up her reserves, and were not averse to stealing.

I could tell that she missed us all, but my little son Christopher more than anyone else, for tears came to her eyes when she told me that in order never to forget she and Martina had christened their latest kitten Christofli. As for Martina, she no longer talked of becoming a nun and I was certain that she would stay around feeding and caring for whatever livestock might be left to them, so long as Frau Muckle was in charge.

But for how long would that be? Only one boy from higher up the valley had returned from the wars to take up his craft as a wheelwright; no further news had reached her after that dreadful day when she heard that her son Ernst was 'missing' and I felt she had given up hope that he would ever return from Russia to take over the inn.

I wished for her so many things, even so far as wishing that I had a son old enough to carry on in Ernst's place.

But after two days I had to leave. I had a long journey before me back to the outside world, a different, for me almost unreal, world, which lay far over the horizon.

Halfway down the hill towards Schönenbach I pulled the jeep over to the side of the track and clambered out.

The snows had left the valley later than last year but cowslips were already pushing their way into the dark patches of pasture left behind.

After removing every spare part which might come in useful the villagers had obviously shown no further interest in the crippled tanks and guns left behind by the retreating German army. Just below me lay one such deserted hulk and again it seemed that only a little bird found it useful for again this year it had decided to build its nest in the exhaust pipe.

As I steered my way down from the hills and back to so-called civilization I was finding it increasingly hard to leave, so that by the time I reached Donaueschingen I decided to postpone my return for just a little longer and head towards Riedlingen and the nearby castle Wilflingen where I hoped to find Dölt and Camilla Stauffenberg, good friends from the Berlin days. Dölt was a cousin of Claus, whose bomb attempt on Hitler's life had so nearly succeeded and Camilla's family came from Northern Ireland; when I had last seen her she had been awaiting Dölt's return from England where he was a prisoner of war.

My transport in those days had been a bicycle and the journey had taken nearly a day, but now behind the wheel of a jeep I managed it in a couple of hours.

They were delighted to see me, particularly because Dölt, who had been released some days before, was enthusiastic about how he had been treated as a POW in England. It was only after my remarking that, in spite of all, I did not think that he was looking particularly healthy that Camilla told me of his fate after leaving England. It would seem that along with other POWs, all of whom had been equally well treated before being sent back home, he had to pass through a British transit camp in Belgium. Here they had all been robbed of their few possessions, their watches, any money, and also practically starved, so that when they had arrived back by the trainload in Düsseldorf many were hardly able to walk. Camilla in her quiet way was obviously embarrassed at telling me this tale and as for me, I was frankly horrified.

On the long journey back to Frankfurt I found myself unable to keep it out of my mind, but as soon as I reached the Press Camp I thought I knew what I should do. I was after all supposed to be a journalist. How should I otherwise be tootling about in a jeep, waving and saluting, with a large golden 'C' on my silly cap? I had a story, I must contact my newspaper immediately.

I was no longer a complete beginner at the game but I thought it best to make an initial tentative approach in order to enquire if it was a story worth developing and, if so, whether they would trust me to carry it further.

If I had ever been in doubt, it was then that I became convinced of the supreme importance of a free press, not to mention in my case, a Foreign Editor bent on upholding liberal and democratic traditions. I was given the go-ahead immediately, and some days later was supplied with the number and location of this camp, the name of the Camp Commandant, and also that of a British Officer who knew of the circumstances and who, after being demobbed, had tried and failed to get any response from the War Office. I was also given an assurance that two Members of Parliament were lined up, ready to put down awkward questions in the House of Commons. One blank that still had to be filled in was to be provided by the War Camps Commission, whose Headquarters were in Berlin. My job was to listen, to record and to assure the Commission that whatever it had to say on the matter would also appear in print.

The Allied train left Frankfurt in the evening, rumbled through the night across what was left of Germany and arrived in Berlin the next morning. Somewhere near Hanover a substantial breakfast was served in a brightly lit restaurant car, and I was only too glad that curtaining covered the lower half of the window, so that those crowding the platforms of every station we passed through could not see what we had on our plates. Eighteen months previously I had been one of them, pushing and scrambling, overtired and hungry, and the journey had taken two days and two nights before we reached our destination. Now a uniform had somehow changed my status, but why that should be the case was sometimes beyond me, for underneath it all, I felt that I was still just me.

I was anxious to get to Berlin, firstly to see if anything was left of our little house in Dahlem, and secondly to discover if there were any friends still left alive in that reportedly devastated city.

As soon as the train reached its destination and came to a steaming halt, a motley crowd pushed forward to the doors and windows, hoping to earn a few cigarettes by carrying any baggage they could lay their hands on. As I stared out over the restless sea of grey faces, I noticed one who was smaller than the rest, less aggressive perhaps. He was wearing a German military cap turned back to front, on which was pinned a large cardboard identity number, very obviously of

77

his own concoction. Despite this personal brain-wave, I could see that due to his size he was gradually losing ground and so, after waiting for the crowd to disperse, I stepped onto the platform and approached him with a request to carry my bag. '*Träger?*' I asked, and was reminded immediately and in no uncertain terms that I was back in Berlin. '*Träyer?*' he piped back as cocky as they come and in that unmistakable Berlin accent which my son John had not lost after months of living in the Black Forest. '*Träyer?* What do you mean? I have been promoted. I am now called, "Porter",' and his pronunciation of the word as he pocketed my packet of Luckys and whipped up my bag could not have been bettered had he been returning from a day's hunting in the Shires.

A message awaited me at the Press Camp that a car would be sent by the POW overlords to fetch me on the following day at eleven o'clock. I had the afternoon to myself and so I decided to make my way to Dahlem and spend some time in our little house there, alone with my memories.

It was summer and the unmistakable smell of pine trees from the *Grünewald* took me back very quickly to those years we spent in the *Falkenried.* As is often the case with memories, in spite of the bombs, the danger, the fears and the sorrows, it was only the happier ones which seemed to be waiting around ready to rise to the surface.

Our little house, which had managed to survive the final onslaught, looked shabby enough, but it was still intact. The garden gate hung askew from one rusty hinge, looking as if someone had given it an almighty kick, and the pathway to the front door was oozing with slippery brown moss. The house seemed to be occupied, however, as my knock was soon answered by an aggressive-looking character in shirt-sleeves, whose expression at the sight of my uniform changed immediately from one of hostility to that mixture of mistrust and servility which I had learned to dislike intensely. Mistrust predominated when I told him in German that I simply wanted to look around, as this had been my home.

From then on, a cloud of almost nightmarish quality went

with me on my tour of inspection. When we had left Berlin many months – it seemed now decades – before, Peter and I had had to abandon most of our possessions: pictures, china, lamps, some furniture, pots and pans. In some way, we had both lost much feeling for possessions, but we were also naïve enough to hope that if a new family took over they would be appreciative of what they found, and take care.

A glance around our sitting-room put an abrupt end to such wishful thinking. It was bare of furniture except for a heavy oak sideboard and an equally heavy oak bridal chest, given to us by Peter's grandmother, peasant furniture from her homeland in Schleswig-Holstein. Highly polished matching suites in rosewood and mahogany were all the rage when we married, but Peter and I loved different things and it seemed to me that there was something essentially reassuring about those sturdy pieces of oak. Wars and invasions had passed over them so often and now they had even succeeded in weathering this latest storm. For the rest, the parquet floors had been ripped up and doubtless used as firewood, and our small collection of Hamburg prints torn from the walls and slashed with knives. There seemed so little point in all this destruction that it was almost a relief to see from the window that our lawn had been dug over to make way for a patch of vegetables.

Meanwhile the man in shirt-sleeves, after shouting up the stairs that there were Americans about the place, had disappeared into our bedroom which was on the ground floor and locked the door behind him.

After leaving the sitting-room, I felt I'd almost had enough. But there was still the door to the cellar where we had stored apples and so often sat together trying to play Snakes and Ladders with the boys during the air raids. So just in case something, a child's toy, anything really, might have managed to remain intact, I opened the door and peered down into the cellar. The stairs were strewn with broken glass and chips of china and at the bottom were the remains of what had once been our household goods and chattels, all smashed to smithereens. I went down the stone steps just in case, and came back up again with an egg cup and a breakfast plate which I wrapped up carefully in my handkerchief before leaving by one of the french windows and pulling shut the garden gate behind me.

An army car came to fetch me at exactly 10.45 a.m. the next morning. Our goal was the Headquarters of the POW Commission. As we wound our way through the narrow canyons which had once been streets, I was given some idea of what had happened to Berlin during those last cataclysmic days when Hitler insisted that it should be defended to the last man.

'I guess the bloody bastard didn't realize what he'd started.' My driver came from Coventry and seemed to have some understanding for the ghostlike figures wandering aimlessly from one pile of rubble to the next. 'Some of the poor buggers don't seem to know where they're going,' he added, as he skilfully avoided one such sleep-walker heading straight for the bonnet of our car.

A pleasant young officer was awaiting our arrival at the bottom of a flight of stone steps which led into one of the few buildings left standing in the street. He escorted me to an antiquated lift which brought us to an upper floor. My hunch that I was being given VIP treatment was confirmed when the door was opened by a busy figure also in uniform; in fact, he was so busy being polite that he obviously did not realize that we had met before. This time he proffered a chair, asked me whether I would care for a cup of coffee, did I smoke, and finally cleared his throat and introduced me to three upright figures of obviously higher rank. They had risen to their feet as I came in and were standing, as if on parade, behind a trestle-table. The table was laden with three massive tomes, one of which was open.

Our conversation began with the usual remarks as to the weather and the pleasantness or otherwise of my journey, until one of the three came to the point and asked if and how they could be of help to me. So I proceeded with my tale, and on being asked if I could identify the camp, I was able to provide them with the details put at my disposal by the *Observer*.

I find there is something straightforward, almost simple, about a high-ranking soldier, from whichever nation he may come. Those before me were particularly good specimens, so that I almost felt sorry for them as they flipped back and forth through the pages of their massive tomes and finally came to rest at one in particular. My instinct told me then that they realized that the game was lost. One indeed asked if the camp were liquidated, would it not be possible for Lord Astor to forget about the whole thing, and here I had to deliver the final blow and tell them that the story would be published the following Sunday and that subsequent questions would be put to the House. Not being used to such things, I found it almost embarrassing to accept their gratitude for being granted space to provide their own version of the story.

Meanwhile, my own little side-show was progressing very favourably. The underling, who was plying me with coffee and cigarettes and had not been asked to take a chair, seemed suddenly to remember that he had seen me some place before. 'Surely, Mrs Bielenberg, we must know each other. I never forget a face,' he murmured in my ear as he put a match to my cigarette. 'Could it have been in London – Paris?' and I could answer coolly, before turning to his superiors, 'Oh yes, we have met, and it wasn't in London or Paris.'

The interview came to an end. 'Take Mrs Bielenberg to the lift, colonel, will you, and see her to her car.'

There is something similar, I discovered, in certain international voices of command which expects immediate obedience and is used to getting it. My companion grabbed my briefcase and leapt for the door, and as he pattered beside me down the long passage which led to the lift, I could sense that he was in no way at ease. 'You know,' he insisted, 'you really have me worried, Mrs Bielenberg. I'm simply quite sure we have met before. Where could it have been?'

I am not by nature a vindictive person, but as I turned to look at him puffing along beside me carrying my briefcase, I could only wonder how often fate allows for such an unexpected day of reckoning.

'You should be worried,' I found myself replying. 'And don't bother to bring me to my car. It was Frankfurt, you see, some months ago, and at the time I was the poor fool who married a bloody German.'

My companion barely reached the lift and I was surely enjoying myself. As the old contraption descended to the ground floor and his head, stocky torso and his boots were cut off from view I realized that I was smiling; a sort of Cheshire Cat smile, and probably not a very nice one I could believe. For, beside my feeling that there was something theatrical about my uniform, I could also rest assured that my farewell message to the POW Camps Commission could be chalked up as a very effective closing line.

It was lunchtime when I returned to the Press Camp and the bar was crowded with journalists, some serious, some lighthearted, few able to speak German, many wearing service ribbons which showed where they had spent the last six years of their lives. They were also generous hearted, only too willing to help an obvious amateur bang the keys and file her story back to London in time for the following Sunday's edition.

'Have a G & T, Chris. You look a bit shattered.' I was not shattered. In fact, after downing a gin and tonic worthy of a confirmed alcoholic, I was decidedly elated. No longer a maverick but a Special Correspondent and, according to those experts, producing front-page stuff, which it proved to be. Now I could take an active part in a different world, perhaps, share the frustrations provided by sub-editors who, according to my companions, had nothing better to do than mangle the literary masterpieces they bashed out so diligently on their ancient typewriters day after day, night after night.

If I allowed my thoughts to wander to the scene outside, news stories were inadequate. Maybe one day I could go one bit further, try to explain and, if possible, make some sense of a theme which would probably never make total sense nor be explained away.

Before leaving Berlin, I had one further obligation to fulfil. It was to discover, if possible, the whereabouts of Alexander Werth. Alexander had been a loyal friend of Adam von Trott, working with him in the German Foreign Office. When a high-up Nazi was put in charge of their department and a bomb destroyed this gentleman's home, Alex offered to take him into his own flat, officially to show willingness, but unofficially to keep an eye on him. Alex himself avoided arrest after the Bomb Plot of 20th July, but fate caught up with him later when he was arrested by the Russians; he was now just another war criminal awaiting trial somewhere in some camp outside Berlin. I decided to try my luck with Alex right away.

It took me some time to persuade one of the taxi-drivers who waited with their ancient vehicles outside the Press Camp every day to take me to the Russian Sector of Berlin. The first one I asked flatly refused, saying that even if he didn't care that much about his life, he did value his taxi. The second seemed to wish that our Eastern Allies had remained on the far side of the Urals, and the third after eyeing my proffered cigarettes, decided to chance it; at least, to get me there as long as I found my own way back. So, to the accompaniment of such ribald comments as, 'See you again some day' and, 'Hope you've got a few sandwiches with you', we set off for Karlshorst where the Russians had established their Headquarters.

We had hardly arrived at a large concrete structure, liberally decorated with hammers and sickles, before my taxi-driver, after wishing me luck, roared off and away in a cloud of dust, as if the devil were on his tail.

A lively throng of men and women in fur caps and shabby tunics were milling about in front of the building, laughing and talking, and as they did so, flashing at all and sundry an extraordinary supply of silver teeth. I did not know whether they were supposed to be guards, but if so, no one seemed to be taking their duty too seriously. In fact, had they been British soldiers, I reckoned only the inevitable football was missing.

Inside the gloomy interior, things seemed slightly more organized. A clerk lounging behind a desk appeared to understand why I was there and directed me up a stone staircase to a small office where an exceptionally good-looking young man with plenty of medals pinned to his tunic greeted me in excellent English. I had come about Alexander Werth, oh yes, he seemed acquainted with the case. He produced a pen made in Germany, offered me a cigarette made in America, listened carefully and proceeded to take down notes.

When I came to the end of my story, he rose to his feet, shook me warmly by the hand, and told me that he himself was not exactly the right person for me to deal with, but if I went along the passage and took the last door on the right, No. 225 – I could not miss it – I would be able to contact the exact official for my needs. I thanked him sincerely, wondering in truth why so much nonsense was being talked about Russian behaviour and inefficiency.

The room number at the end of the passage which he had given me proved to be a large hall completely void of furniture, except for rows of wooden chairs placed around the walls. They were occupied by chattering boys and girls, all in uniform, who seemed to move along in pairs from one chair to the next, until they reached the door at the far end when they disappeared behind it. After some minutes they reappeared through another door to be greeted with much laughter and back-slapping, so obviously delighted with each other's company.

There were no officials to be seen and, as everyone was speaking Russian, when I sat myself down at the end of the queue it took me some little time to make out what was going on. The wrong room? That could not be possible, for the handsome officer had definitely said the last one on the right and given me its number.

I was nearing the far door and the couple ahead of me were obviously becoming more excited and fidgety by the minute before I realized what might be happening and got up to leave. Whatever was going on behind that door had definitely nothing to do with Alexander Werth. In fact, I decided that it must be some kind of marriage registry and the absurd thought ran through my mind that if I stayed any longer I might find myself bigamously married to a Russian.

A quick visit back down the passage was enough to convince me that my self-appointed mission to help Alex had been a complete fiasco. No one was about; I was greeted with echoing silence, and the door to the office of my handsome Russian officer was firmly locked.

When I got outside the building an overcrowded tram was preparing to leave and a long queue was already forming, doubtless in the hope of getting the next one.

As we moved forward step by step I found myself standing beside a tall slight girl who looked in some way different from the shapeless human bundles who were shuffling along beside us. She was not lugging the inevitable bulging sack, and her clothes were dark green; from Bavaria I could imagine for, although they were shabby and well worn, they were unmistakably well cut. 'I wish you had hurried along just that bit faster last year.' The voice beside me seemed to be directed at the ample back of the lady in front of us, but, to my surprise, was speaking English, which could only be meant for me. 'How do you mean? The Allies? The advance on Berlin? If so, I couldn't agree more,' I replied with some feeling, thinking of those days back in the Black Forest when we could only pray that the final storm would pass over us as soon as possible and leave us alive. The girl was now looking at me with a smile, a sad sort of half-smile, but she seemed to want to go on talking, to unburden herself maybe, in a language that only I could understand. 'Just another fifty kilometres, you see, and we could have welcomed everyone to my home. Instead—'

A tram came rattling down the track towards us and it was not until we found ourselves propelled inside and wedged in next to each other that she could continue. Instead – well, instead it had of course been the Russians, and her father could not bring himself to leave his lands. Her mother had died during the war and both her brothers had been killed on the Eastern Front. So, without his lands, without an heir, he had no particular reason for wanting to live anyway. No one had heard the shot with which her father had killed himself, for the Russians were practically at the gates by then and a lot of shooting was going on in the village. But a faithful gamekeeper had seen to it that the Herr Graf had a proper burial, whatever that might mean. 'Under one of his trees, I hope, I never had the courage to go and see.'

As for herself, she had been extraordinarily lucky. In true Prussian fashion, her parents always insisted that she spend certain days of the year in the kitchen quarters, learning to cook, learning to cope with the quantities of meat — hams and sausages — which needed smoking, and preparing to see the household through the winter; learning to get to know those who worked on the Estate, their *Leute*, their people, as she called them.

When the Russians finally burst in she retired to the kitchens, and although the work was hard enough, she was not molested nor did she starve, for the cook was a natural martinet and soon managed to convince even the Russian soldiery of the need for orderly behaviour. 'No proper manners — no food' and that was that!

Luck, too, was on her side when the Russian commandant who held the rank of colonel moved in later with his wife and two children — a boy and a girl — and she was promoted to playing the role of governess. 'It was an extraordinary experience really, because although the children were not easy to teach — already somehow too spoilt — their parents were ardent learners and never failed to turn up every evening with their homework neatly completed.'

Her colonel and his family were now stationed in Berlin and had decided to bring her along with them. Beside the cooking and the cleaning and the supervising of their education, she was at present engaged in a rather bizarre extra task.

It would seem that one of the perks granted to a Russian

Christabel, 1940.

My father and mother, Colonel Percy Burton and Christabel née *Harmsworth.*

WEDDING OF PEER'S NIECE

The big decision: 29 September 1934. Peter's and my marriage in the Marylebone Register Office.

Bride and bridegroom after the wedding, at Marylebone register office yesterday, of Miss Christabel Burton, elder daughter of Major and Mrs. P. C Burton and niece of Lord Rothermere, with Mr. Peter Bielenberg, only son of Mr and Mrs. Bielenberg, of Hamburg.

Our house in Berlin – the only one in the district which remained completely intact.

Christopher with his only toy at the time – a lemonade bottle. Rohrbach, 1945.

Nicky and Christopher watching Allied planes flying over Rohrbach en route to Munich.

The rubble women of Berlin, who, to my mind, laid the foundations of Germany's future prosperity.

Peter with one of the first lambs born on our farm.

Christopher with his pet lamb, 1951.

1950: John on board the tractor, his over-riding passion.

Clarita von Trott with her two daughters, Verena and Adi, myself, Nicky and Christopher on the steps of our house in Ireland.

Our three sons, Nicky, John and Christopher, on holiday in Killarney, 1953.

Munny House after a certain amount of rehabilitation.

(© David Gamble)

Myself and Peter at Munny.

At Munny, 1985.

officer was permission for his eldest son to wear an identical uniform, medals included, but, of course, in miniature. Father though had noticed that his offspring was not taking sufficient care of his get-up and came to the conclusion that the mess down the front must come about because of his son's habit of blowing his nose out of the window instead of using a handkerchief.

So *Fräulein* was summoned and expected to go into action. 'They didn't seem to have any handkerchiefs,' she explained, so, 'right nostril, foof — left nostril, faf.' My companion could not suppress a real laugh as she described her ultimate expertise in directing the seemingly endless flow of snot emitted by her charge; 'Out of the window, but not into the wind!' had been her solution.

The girl left the tram before it clattered its way out of the Russian Sector and into the British. As I watched her through the window, pushing her way resolutely along the crowded pavement, it occurred to me that although we had talked together in much harmony, I had not asked her name, nor she mine. Old habits die hard, for me as well as for her. We had been through so many years when mere acquaintanceship was simply not enough, could even be dangerous. It had to be friendship, real friendship, before the barriers fell.

After some months, Alex Werth was freed from captivity, and, being a truthful man, had to tell me that my visit had been of little help to him — in fact, to the contrary. The atmosphere between us and our Eastern Allies was no longer a warm one, it would seem, and in fact, my plea on his behalf had merely aroused extra suspicion.

Chapter Seven

Iт тоок several months before Freda's urgent advice to get Peter out soonest could materialize. My father was particularly active on our behalf which I found very touching especially when I remembered his original anxiety about our marriage. Friends, too, helped wherever possible, but Allied directives were strict and the year was nearing its end before I could return to that Kronberg kitchen waving a travel permit to England for Peter H. W. Bielenberg, Doctor of Law. It was the first of its kind to be issued to a German civilian after hostilities ceased.

So much for the hopes of all those love-lorn German females Freda was so bothered about, that was a party! Hans and Ellen Eiche arrived with two bottles of superb Alsatian wine which they had discovered in father Eiche's cellar. They also had every reason to be cheerful because their little girl, Ursula, had recovered from meningitis after an American army doctor had provided me with penicillin which was otherwise unobtainable except on the black market, where the going rate per shot was an unobtainable ten kilos of butter. Bob Stephens of the *Observer*, Betty, Dick and Pat Nicholson, two other American officers and two from UNRRA, also armed with bottles, all seemed happy enough to forgo some PX meal and share with us an extraordinary mixture which Freda and I managed to cook up with everything we could find in the larder.

Some weeks earlier Peter had resigned from the De-Nazification Board without bloodshed and moved to the newly established Board of Trade, and, on hearing the good news, made a dash for the black market, spent a fortune and returned with a spectacular bottle of what was supposedly vintage brandy but which turned out to be cold tea. But nothing could dampen our spirits; even Hannes, Freda's husband, was persuaded to leave his philosophical studies in peace for an hour or so. He had been freed from jail in the summer after some effort I had made on his behalf and had since been banished to the attic along with a gim-crack typewriter which got on everyone's nerves but his own.

It was surely a good party and not without temporary drama for, doubtless due to those unaccustomed bottles, before it broke up there was some confusion as to the exact whereabouts of Peter's precious travel permit.

I knew that I could not stay in Frankfurt for long because just before leaving England a situation had arisen which I had seen coming all summer. Needless to say, it concerned my little son Christopher and his so-called watchdog Madi. Madi had managed to survive my absence in the spring but, on hearing that I might be away again and possibly for a week or so, she clutched her ample bosom and nearly had a heart attack on the spot.

My sister and I had done our best to postpone the day of decision by carting all the children off to Devonshire during the holidays in order to spend a fortnight by the sea in pouring rain. I would have preferred to take the children to Ireland, not because of the lashings of bacon and eggs and soda bread which were luring ration-weary Britons in droves to cross the Irish Sea, but simply because of my nostalgic memories of a happy-go-lucky island which belonged to my own carefree childhood. But back here in Codicote, having witnessed Madi chasing the little darling around the garden at lunchtime, teatime and bedtime, I was not really surprised when a week before I left she packed her bags and made her tearful goodbyes.

I know that I have a habit of leaving possible problems until the last moment, always hoping that some wonderful solution will come to my rescue but, beyond cutting myself in half, on this occasion I could find none. In fact, as the day for my departure drew nearer I was ready to stuff Christopher into my duffel bag and take him along with me, when my brother John, who had unbearable memories of public school, came up with a possible answer: A. S. Neill's boarding-school in Somerset where the Founder and Head Master was a pioneer in the science of education, allowing the pupils in his care to do more or less exactly as they liked whenever they pleased.

My interview with Mr Neill took place in his so-called office, seated on a three-legged sofa only kept on an even keel by a pile of books. He explained that the missing leg was the result of a minor revolution which had taken place in the school the term before, when some of the older boys had gone on the rampage, smashing windows, breaking crockery and chopping up their desks and beds. His response had been to provide panes of glass and planks of wood and leave them to repair the damage themselves which, as the days grew colder and their discomfort more acute, he assured me they had managed most successfully. He also assured me that the Junior School was still intact and on my rather dubious tour of inspection I found this to be the case: a warm comfortable little house with plenty of toys about the place and a gentle nanny-like matron whom I trusted on first sight.

So Neill's school it was to be and thus Christopher took his first step on an unusual journey through eleven different schools before arriving sixteen years later at an Honours Degree in the Sciences at Trinity College, Dublin. I still wonder whether this unorthodox approach to a gratifying conclusion, although partly due to circumstances, did not also include my own indecision as a parent, after having

90

the iniquity of the traditional educational system explained to me in much detail while sitting on a three-legged sofa in Somerset.

But all this, as the Germans would say, was *Zukunftsmusik* – future music. For the time being it was 1946, I was in Frankfurt muddling my way along through clouds of uncertainties, and besides being the bearer of good tidings I had two further reasons for being there.

Firstly, as the weeks went by, it had become clear to all concerned that our fund to help the widows of the 20th July Bomb Plot was getting completely out of hand. Gritta could hardly get into her little office for the piles of parcels which were piling up daily, and poor Diana's typewriter was working overtime. We had asked Marion Dönhoff, a good friend of ours, to help from the German end, but she was starting up a newspaper and had hinted that she could no longer carry on. We would have to find someone else.

My second reason could become a little more complicated. It concerned a certain Gerhard Graf von Schwerin whom David had heard was in an American prison camp awaiting trial as a war criminal.

We had known Graf von Schwerin since before the war when, a young officer in the *Wehrmacht*, he crossed to England in order, as he hoped, to warn the British of what lay ahead should Hitler remain in power. He had not been alone in his belief that the British, instead of continuously negotiating *à la* Munich, should be persuaded to make some dramatic gesture. An envoy, preferably a general, should be sent by the King direct to Hitler in person, bypassing diplomatic channels, and carrying with him a simple message, 'One more move and it's war!'.

It was, of course, questionable whether such a warning would have caused Hitler to hesitate, but there were many who thought it worth a try. Indeed, some days before war actually broke out, Peter had pocketed his call-up papers and set off for England carrying the same desperate last-minute plea. Both Peter and Schwerin returned empty-handed: Schwerin, because the British High Command seemed to suspect something treacherous in his behaviour; Peter, because it was August and most responsible civil servants were away on holiday.

We had not seen much of Schwerin during the war as he seldom came to Berlin on leave, but it was not difficult to follow his career as he was transferred from battlefield to battlefield and was promoted to Major-General. This was because of the unofficial dispatches he sent to trusted friends on the home front. From Poland, from France, from Russia and finally from Italy, Schwerin minced no words describing conditions existing at the front, never attempting to hide his intense disapproval of excesses he believed to be prevailing behind the battle-lines. He was, in fact, one of those courageous and highly efficient professional soldiers who had found themselves caught in a dilemma, that of fighting for an overlord whose methods of warfare they knew to be despicable.

On his pre-war mission to England Schwerin had met with and sought help from David Astor, not so well known to me at the time, but someone I was learning to appreciate warmly as a friend who would never give up. David had trusted and liked Schwerin, who was now in Dachau, a former concentration camp transformed by the Americans into an internment camp for major war criminals awaiting trial.

There must be some mistake — something must be done. When it came to the value of friendship and to the possibility of injustice David was like a hound on the trail. So, although I could hardly believe that a practically unknown British war correspondent would find it easy to barge her way unaided into such a fortress and persuade whoever was in charge as to the wrongness of their ways, I knew the very least I could do was to give it a try.

When we discussed how best to start off on such a venture, Captain Register immediately came to mind and I remembered how he had stressed the importance of a rubber stamp when dealing with the Army; it was not long before David came up trumps with something even better. This was a letter of introduction and a request for assistance to my humble self, signed by Robert Murphy, Political Advisor to General Eisenhower.

This trip to Dachau had to be my first priority and as soon as Pat Nicholson could provide suitable transport, even including a chauffeur when she read my credentials and I told her of my goal, I left Frankfurt for Munich. By then, I was already armed with two further letters from amiable generals who had taken note of Robert Murphy's signature and seen no harm in joining in.

My only experience of a concentration camp had been Ravensbrück where I had visited Peter in 1944. I was to discover that Dachau, even under new management, was just as sinister. The high wire fence with its watch-guard towers, the Nissen huts, all looked as if they had been there for a long time. Only guards in black battle-dress with MP blazoned in white on their steel helmets were more recent arrivals. As in Ravensbrück, the Camp Commandant had taken up residence outside the camp's perimeter and I experienced a strange sensation of *déjà vu* when I rang the doorbell of a neat villa and the door was opened by a short fattish man with a cold blue eye and a shaven head. He was wearing a pair of the most highly polished army boots I had ever seen in my life. Why those boots and leather gaiters made such an impression I do not know, for it did not take long to discover that despite a certain swagger of authority, he was not too sure what to do with me once he had read my letters of introduction. His frequent irresolute glances at the badge on my cap betrayed the typical response of all underlings whose common sense tells them to do one thing, but whose fear of reprimand from above causes them to do another. But it gave me much satisfaction that he did not seem to recognize the golden 'C' as being connected with the Press.

It would be wrong to pretend that my interview with Dachau's Camp Commandant caused me much misgiving. In fact, by the time he agreed to grant me a ten-minute interview with Schwerin, I was almost beginning to enjoy myself. It was hardly possible to believe that little more than a year had passed

since I sat, numb with fear, awaiting my turn in the Prinz
Albrechtstrasse Headquarters of the Gestapo; the scenario was
so similar but the circumstances so very different. When we
parted, a jeep manned by several guards was waiting to take
me on my journey into the camp. Bulging rolls of barbed wire
hedged us in as we wound our way from one narrow track to the
next before arriving at what seemed the very centre of the
enclosure. An open space, a parade ground perhaps, surrounded
by the inevitable Nissen huts, with no sound coming from their
boarded walls and wired-up windows, except from one where
black-clad guards lounged about on the steps in the sun, and
a radio squawked in the background.

The guards were obviously forewarned of my arrival, and
the fact that one came forward to help me out of the jeep
seemed to indicate that the commandant had failed to judge
the insignificance of my rank or to make out the reason for my
presence.

'Prisoner No. 75 will be over any moment,' I was told, and
it was not long before an upright figure wearing one of those
white sheepskin greatcoats provided (as often as not too late)
for the German troops in Russia, emerged from between two
of the distant huts and walked briskly towards us, carrying his
cap under his arm.

'At last a general that looks like a general,' drawled one of
the guards who was watching Schwerin's approach, and as he
had just informed me that he sure liked my English brogue,
I felt that things so far were not going too badly at all. However, one thing that I had not reckoned with was the profound
shock my appearance would have on poor Gerhard. The last
time we had met was in Berlin. He had been wearing civilian
clothes which smelled strongly of mothballs and he had offered to
hang them in the garden and borrow some things of Peter's for
the afternoon. Now, having nodded to the guards and placed
his cap (from which I noticed all insignia had been removed)
on the table beside the door, his glance passed to me and he
froze. For one dreadful moment I thought he might burst
out, 'Chris! *Um Gottes Willen!*' or some such inappropriate

greeting. But I suppose he had been a prisoner long enough, for he merely stood there silently, staring at me as if at a ghost, whilst sudden beads of perspiration appeared on his forehead, cheeks and chin.

'Ten minutes – OK?' The tension was broken by one of the guards, and I could help out a little by addressing him formally in German.

'Graf Schwerin, I have been given ten minutes in which to discuss certain matters with you,' I said. Then, realizing that we might not be able to keep up this formality for long, and also that my confidence was growing by the minute, I turned to the guards and announced in my best 'English brogue' that I wished, of course, to speak with the General in private.

No one seemed to object, and we were ushered into a small adjoining room not much bigger than a cupboard, where the furniture consisted of a bench against the wall, and the décor was provided by a poster displaying two completely naked ladies laughing and waving, seated astride a bored-looking giraffe. The bench was needed by both of us because when Gerhard turned to take my hand, I realized that he was near to tears and his voice had almost deserted him. Finally, he managed to bring out, 'I'm sorry, Chris, what a welcome – but I had no warning – thought I was being summoned to an interrogation, and then you of all people – a friend and in British uniform. I'm really sorry.' Then, pulling himself together, he straightened his back and burst out, '*Um Gottes Willen!* Am I mad? What are you doing in this dump?'

'You're not a bit mad,' I assured him. 'It's just something that's wrong with the world.' And in order to give him time, I thought it well to repeat the remark the guard had made about him as he crossed the parade ground. Then, realizing that the precious minutes were passing, I hurried on to ask him whether in heaven's name he had any idea why he was there.

'I have none whatsoever,' he replied. 'I just know that I go from one interrogation to the next – no ill treatment, mind you – but just the same questions over and over again about places and happenings I know nothing about. I tell them so and I know they don't believe me. One of them even told me he'd like to meet the Kraut who knew anything about anything, and as far as he was concerned the whole race was a bunch of bloody liars. Now they've got stuck into a case where five hostages from some village near Brussels were shot on my express orders and I was never near the place. It's degrading – how could . . .?' Gerhard jumped to his feet, and if the room had not been so small, I felt he would have started pacing up and down.

It was then that for me things started to fall into place. Gerhard was a professional soldier, equipped with all the nobler attributes of his class and profession and also some of the limitations. I could imagine that he was making a glorious mess of his interrogations because he knew he was telling the truth, was being dubbed a liar, and this was hitting him so hard that he was becoming almost incapable of defending himself.

'Listen, Gerhard,' I said. 'We're getting nowhere this way, and we haven't much time left. If you weren't where they think you were, are there any other Schwerins about the place?'

'Oh, yes,' he replied, 'there are lots of us around. We are a big clan.'

'No one in the SS, I suppose?' My innocent question almost seemed to make him jump, but he answered quietly, 'Yes, unfortunately, one.' And, as if still not understanding the importance of what he was saying, he added, 'I did not know him nor wish to know him. He may in fact be dead.'

'Good God, Gerhard!' Had it not been for the guards next door, I would have been shouting. 'Can't you see, dead or alive, he's the answer? Quickly – his name. It's mistaken identity.' I was almost stuttering with excitement as I gave him my notebook and he began to write down a name very slowly, much too slowly, as if almost ashamed at having to do so.

I could hear chairs being scraped back along the floor of the room next door as I opened my briefcase to stow away this precious document. It was then that I came across the five cartons of cigarettes I had brought with me in case of emergency. I had forgotten about them – how maddening – and now it was too late.

But I had not reckoned with a newly resurrected Graf von Schwerin, and it was my turn to be amazed.

'Quickly, can you . . .?'

'Can I not?' he answered briskly, and in a matter of seconds he stuffed two cartons down each sleeve of his sheepskin greatcoat and one into his belt and was standing before me as if he had not moved a muscle. As the door opened and a guard called out that our time was up, Gerhard was grinning like a schoolboy and managed, in spite of the stuffing, to bow and kiss my hand.

'Goodbye, Mrs Bielenberg, and thank you,' he said, and added in English, before leaving on what I felt might be a chancy crossing of the parade ground, 'at last a General who knows what he's doing.'

Some six weeks later, a long letter from Gerhard von Schwerin was left for me at the Press Camp. He had been released from Dachau and was driving trucks for the Americans. He seemed to think that I had played some part in saving his life, but I knew that without that inimitable rubber stamp, I would have got nowhere, and he might still be shut up in Dachau, wondering why.

After what I hoped had been a worthwhile effort I still had one more task to fulfil before I could leave Germany, and as Peter, too, had to sort some things out before retiring from the Board of Trade, I decided to head off for Hamburg and discuss the future of our 20th July Memorial Fund with Marion Dönhoff herself. I found her in fine fettle as her newspaper, *Die Zeit*, which appeared once a week was already becoming well established. The first edition had indeed been a complete sell-out and the enthusiasm of her colleagues was only slightly tempered when they were informed in true Hamburg fashion (Hamburg being a city where high spirits are not really approved of) that this initial success was not surprising as they happened to have chosen a day when the fish market was doing business and, wrapping paper being

97

scarce or non-existent, they could reckon for themselves what use had been made of their literary efforts. The name she gave me was of a Graf Hardenberg who was the administrator of the Hohenzollern Estates. I was frankly a little surprised that such things still existed, for having been a small child in the First World War and having burned the effigy of the Kaiser every Guy Fawkes' Day during my childhood, I thought we must have got rid of the Hohenzollerns and their possessions for good and all. But it seemed that Graf Hardenberg's wife was showing lively interest in the 20th July Memorial Fund and the address Marion gave me in order to contact her was in Berlin, from whence it would seem her husband administered whatever remained of the Kaiser's goods and chattels. I decided, therefore, to make straight for Berlin before returning to Frankfurt.

In the *Reichstrümmerstadt* (State Rubble Town), after wandering up and down several nameless alleyways, unoccupied, except for where an unexpected chimney thrust its nose through the rubble, and drifting smoke seemed to indicate that human beings could be living underneath, searching for the address Marion had given me, I decided I must have been right about the Kaiser, or at least he must have moved house. I was, therefore, taken aback when, passing the shattered remains of a tree, I saw a neat notice pinned to its stump: No. 75. There could be no doubt about it, nor about the arrow pointing to the left at what seemed to be just another mountain of bricks and mortar.

On closer examination, I discovered that the arrow was pointing towards a narrow passage, skilfully cleared of rubble and laid down with paving stones from which every speck of dust had been brushed. By the time the twists and turns brought me to a highly polished door and a radiant brass plate indicated that I had reached my destination, I was ready for almost anything, although hardly for my tentative knock to be answered immediately by a spruce figure whose glossy shaven pate was devoid of hair except for a neat tuft on the top which was parted expertly down the middle. He was wearing some kind of uniform which included highly polished leather gaiters and white cotton gloves.

'The *gnädige Frau* is expected and is welcome,' he announced, addressing me in the third person, which I seemed to remember as being a somewhat out-dated procedure still preferred by the more die-hard members of German nobility when being spoken to by an underling.

'Would the *gnädige Frau* take a chair? Would she care for a cup of tea?' As he ushered me into a small dark room and steered me towards two chairs and a large refectory table which seemed to complete the furnishing, little did he know that he could have added, 'And would the *gnädige Frau* now like to get the shock of a lifetime?' For, when bustling off to a further door telling me that he intended alerting the *Herr Graf* of my arrival, he reached up in passing and pulled on a piece of cord which had the instant effect of flooding the room with bright light. The transformation did not come from above me, but, to my horror, from a full-length, fully illuminated wall portrait of *Seine Kaiserliche Hoheit* himself – Kaiser Bill – Big Willie, the bogeyman of my early childhood. There he was, just as I had known as a child he would be, with his golden eagle atop a brass helmet, his white uniform ablaze with coloured sashes and brassy medals, but, above all, his cadaverous face, his cold brown staring eyes and his moustache trimmed like the letter 'W'. No wonder I had never dared have a bath on my own in those days of my childhood for there was always that narrow space between the bath-tub and the wall, and who could promise me that one bath-night the dreaded monster might not manage to ooze his way up it, helmet and all, before I could grab my towel and make for the nursery!

A ghost was laid when Graf Hardenberg appeared and proved to be a tall, slight, very gentle person. He did not look well fed, his clothes hung loosely about him and one empty sleeve was tucked into his jacket pocket. But he was genuinely grateful that such a fund as ours had been started, and for him it was nothing less than miraculous that the response from ordinary English people had been so immediate. He knew that his wife, who had many personal friends among the widows of those who had been hanged after the failure of the 20th July Plot, would be overjoyed to play her part. Such was his enthusiasm that when I got up to leave, I was convinced that our somewhat amateur venture at reconciliation was worthwhile, and almost felt like cocking a well-deserved snook at Big Willie, who, during our talk together, had remained immobile, staring sternly down over his countryman's shoulder, as if rigid with disapproval.

Graf Hardenberg took me to the door, apologizing for being unable to accompany me further. As we stood in the doorway, a shaft of evening sun lit up the ruins about us, casting weird silhouettes against the clear Berlin sky. A windowless wall, a rickety chimney stack like a hunchback cripple, looking down over huge grey boulders which might have belonged to some retreating mountain glacier. 'We Germans have got to calling this time, *Die Stunde Null* – zero hour,' my companion remarked as he kissed my hand and asked that God might bless our efforts. Then he added with a sudden smile, 'But maybe our meeting here has started something new. Let's call it from now on *Die Stunde Eins*.'

When I arrived back at the shattered tree stump, the sun had set, evening was closing in and a rather beautiful pink glow lit up the stark outlines of the rubble summits, last to catch the evening light against the still cloudless sky.

As I set off rather hesitantly back down the pathway I had come by, I was beginning to wonder how I was going to find my way out of this silent moon-world before darkness fell. I was therefore much relieved when movement of a kind, accompanied by a curious rhythmic clanking, materialized out of the shadows ahead of me. I quickened my step but had no need to hurry in order to catch up with a line of marching figures. It was difficult at first to tell if they were men or women for some were shouldering spades, some pick-axes, and shapeless sacking seemed to play a major role in whatever they were wearing. Nor would marching be the right word to describe their progress, although they seemed to be shuffling their way forward in some kind of rhythm, banging the buckets which formed part of their equipment against the path's side walls. I did not want to push past them and seeing that they were obviously heading for some place and I was lost, I decided to tag along behind and hope for the best.

We came to a second rather more important crossing where one or two broke away from the group and, murmuring something which sounded like, 'Good night – 'till tomorrow', they made off down one of the side-tracks of which I counted five in all. Five gaping holes in the rubble walls, five possibilities of taking a wrong turn – I decided that the moment had come for me to explain myself.

I was an alien in their midst, but I could speak German and my lack of any air of authority was so manifest that in spite of my uniform they gathered around me, obviously eager to be of help.

At close quarters there was no mistaking that my companions were all women. The drab headgear, caps and scarves and shapeless lumps of felt, and the rest of their rig-out – a hotch-potch of any old remnants capable of being used as protection against the elements – could have belonged to either sex, but their voices were women's voices, their hands were women's hands as they leaned on their shovels and proceeded to bombard me in a variety of dialects of which I could only recognize that of Berlin.

Where was I going? They, as I could see, were on their way to the Opera – *Rosenkavalier* – pass the chocolates, Irmgard! As usual it was a chirpy Berliner amongst them who was guaranteed to raise a laugh. The fact that I was billeted in a part of Berlin taken over by the British caused some confusion, and a waving of picks and shovels in all directions gave me to understand that they hadn't a clue how to get there. Confined as they were to their own bit of ground, the rest of Berlin was plainly unknown territory.

By the time a heated argument amongst themselves as to my future was well under way, some of the manifestly exhausted ladies were already giving themselves a much needed rest on their upturned buckets, others had flopped to the ground and, seated with their backs to the walls, were staring dully at their unwieldy old boots.

Something told me that this might be the moment to produce some cigarettes. The Kaiser had managed to keep me off them all day and with luck I had enough for all of us. 'Listen,' I said as loudly as I could above the clamour, 'you are just being too kind, too solicitous. Why don't I tag along with you until we meet up with a main road, and maybe a tram or a taxi or even a military vehicle might be passing and you can push me into it and get rid of me. But in the meantime, why don't we smoke a cigarette together?' 'A cigarette?', 'One each?' A deep, almost reverent silence descended immediately, not, I knew, because of my brilliant solving of their problem, but at the sound of that sacred word, cigarette – Holy Writ! – and as I went the rounds with my lighter, watching the look of complete contentment which came over one dusty face after another, I decided that in the future no one was going to persuade me that cigarettes were bad for you.

As we sat there puffing away in the half-light, watched over by the towering ruins, I was able to listen to some of the stories they had to tell. There were refugees from the East amongst them, some who could barely speak German, although most of them were from Berlin, and two came from Dresden. None of them seemed really young any more and the tales they told were grimly repetitive. The long trek westwards driven from their homes like cattle, husbands dead or missing, children lost, and then those final days and nights in Berlin, the howling shells, the seething flames, as they prayed in vain that the Allies would arrive before the Russians. Lastly, the violation, the rape, some not once, not twice, but many times. The Russians were being allowed to take their revenge and the sagas which unfolded were horrific, somehow made even more so by the absence of self-pity, the almost matter-of-fact way in which they were told.

Time was passing, cigarettes ceased to glow, although I noticed that the stubs were being carefully stowed away in apron pockets. The day was not yet over for my companions: some had to fetch children from friends or relatives who looked after them during the day, others to join long queues for possible food or firing for themselves and for others too old or too ill to manage. Each to her appointed task; they had learned the value of teamwork in the survival game.

The journey to the main road did not take too long. We seemed to be moving more swiftly and the faces about me suddenly looked much younger.

I have a theory that women, old school-friends, old buddies, when they get together and feel so inclined, are ready to cast their years and responsibilities to the winds and become quite juvenile. Why this should be I do not know, but it was so when one of us noticed that the jagged cliffs about us, if given some encouragement, could return a resounding echo and, before we knew quite what we were about, this had us cooing and crowing, booing and bawling and hardly able to control ourselves with laughter, waiting for the answer to float back at us from the non-existent roof-tops. We were thoroughly enjoying ourselves and the game would have gone on longer if one voice had not decided to shout, '*Heil!*' and, as '*Heil*' after '*Heil*' came back at us, the fun was suddenly over and we were reduced to silence. So much for memories. '*Ein kleiner Schönheitsfehler* – a bit of a mistake,' remarked my neighbour, wiping away the tears of laughter with her apron. 'I guess she meant to yell out *Hölle* (Hell).'

The driver and the conductor and most of the passengers on the rickety old tram which picked me up at the main road were also women, and after waving goodbye to the last few stalwarts who had insisted on coming with me to the tram stop, it occurred to me that during the time we had been together, talked and laughed together, hardly any mention had been made of the male sex. Distant memories of ladies' tea parties came flooding back to me when, 'I must ask my husband', was a constant battle squeak, and when over-worked fathers, equally over-worked husbands, and their resultant 'nerves' supplied an endless subject for conversation. I had been new to the role of *Hausfrau* then and it remained a mystery to me how German women, whose efficiency I envied, could succumb so easily to second-class citizenship.

Now, after six years of war and a year of so-called liberation, these same women had carried on scrimping and saving, foraging for food, managing to keep their families alive, the remains of their homes intact. Could it be they had discovered that they could do so quite successfully on their own? Soon what was left of their menfolk would be drifting homewards and I could only wonder if they would be allowed to slip back into their old-established roles as undisputed masters of the household.

Back in the comparatively supreme comfort of the Press Camp where we could indulge in plenty of complaints about the dullness of the NAAFI food, and the lumpy mattresses which reminded us all of boarding-school, I found my thoughts returning to those *Trümmerfrauen* – the Rubble Women. These were the German women whom Hitler had identified with his famous three 'Ks' – *Kinder, Küche, Kirche* – children, the kitchen and the church – and here they were, dusty and dishevelled but undaunted, replacing their missing menfolk, clearing up, starting again at the beginning. *Die Stunde Null*, zero hour. If ever there was to be a start somewhere, it seemed to me that with their dusty faces, calloused hands and ragged aprons, these women could certainly count themselves among the flag bearers of *Die Stunde Eins*.

Three days after my return to Frankfurt from Berlin, Peter and I left for England. Only allied personnel could travel by air and the rail route prescribed for us was via Hanover, Hamburg and Copenhagen. Just before leaving, an envelope marked, 'On His Majesty's Service' was delivered at the Press Camp. My passport, and although I was described inside as a naturalized British subject of British birth and, though I could not quite understand how I could have managed to become both, I was only too happy to welcome the lion and the unicorn back into my possession once more.

As soon as we crossed the Danish border I removed my uniform and became myself again, although I cannot pretend that the rather weary eight-year-old garment which I had brought with me from Kronberg would stamp me as travelling in the height of fashion.

In Copenhagen we headed for one of our pre-war favourite restaurants where Peter demolished a huge basin of *Bœuf Stroganoff* and I nearly managed to clear the most extensive platter of smoked salmon I had ever set eyes on.

I do not know why but, during the long train journey through devastated Germany and then Denmark, where the villages and little towns showed no bomb scars whatsoever, Graf Hardenberg's farewell words to me in Berlin kept recurring in my mind. *Die Stunde Null* – zero hour – was easy enough to translate, but what about *Die Stunde Eins*. It was only on the following morning when Peter and I were leaning on the ship's rails as dawn was breaking that I thought to have found an answer.

Die Stunde Eins, why try to translate the words? Let them simply remain a symbol of hope for two young human beings with lots of life before them, leaning over those railings in the early dawn and wondering what lay ahead as the ship left the North Sea storms behind and glided smoothly into the mouth of the Thames.

Chapter Eight

I HAVE COME to believe that as a lifetime progresses, it does so from one milestone to the next. You may think to be following a certain course, but unseen, unrecognizable as such at the time, events lie ahead waiting for you to come their way and stop short before passing by.

Thoughts such as these kept churning over in my mind as night after night I sat at Peter's bedside in the casualty ward of Selly Oak Hospital, in Birmingham, waiting and hoping for him to regain consciousness.

It seemed so useless to ask why this essential part of my life should have survived the war, the bombs, the dangers and months in a concentration camp and now lie here motionless, looking so young, breathing so lightly, maybe slipping away without protest into the unknown. Useless to ask why had it to be, that just as some kind of future, however uncertain, seemed to be dawning on our horizon, a motor cycle, a careless lorry driver and a fractured skull should have been allowed to block our path and bring us to possible finality, an unforeseen, inescapable cul-de-sac. The surgeon had asked me was Peter's heartbeat by nature very slow – an athlete's heart? — yes, yes, it was! My answer seemed to please him. He was an honest man just out of the Army and obviously accustomed to giving a forthright opinion. In that case he could raise my hopes from a 10 per cent to a 20 per cent chance of recovery. What exactly he meant by 'recovery' I had not dared to ask.

A hospital ward is an eerie place at night, when the rattling trolleys and all other daytime commotion have died away, when the lights are dimmed, and the nurses move from bed to bed like wraiths on their slippered feet. Only an occasional sigh, a whimper or perhaps a moan breaks the silence as one or other would-be survivor lies there struggling, however feebly, to cling on to life. When left so alone in a twilight world with no reliable future ahead of me, I found it easier to live with memories of the past. There was certainty, happiness, even a few absurdities about the past which were all safer to think about than a future which did not bear thought. I had many such memories to call upon.

There was, for instance, the tumultuous reception given to Peter by my family, all obviously determined to make it extra special. My father, returning from the cellar with some superb bottles and my mother, after clearing the garden of flowers, throwing her principles to the winds, and managing to rustle up a beef roast of pre-war dimensions. Peter, my brothers, my brother-in-law and a favourite cousin, not yet out of uniform, five young men all able to make nonsense of six years of bitter enmity by the warmth of their welcome and their obvious pleasure at still being alive and able to meet up with each other once again.

Then there was the day I set off for Neill's school in Somerset to discover how Christopher was faring in his educational establishment. I went on my own as, after our long separation, I was not too certain whether Peter who, just as I had been months before, was being confronted by new impressions every day, might not find this particular phenomenon on the post-war English scene to be well beyond his understanding. True enough, I found Christopher squatting on the floor of a large bare gym hall amongst other little boys, some of whom were smoking cigarettes.

There are certain unforgettable moments in life and one must be when you know for certain that you are loved, loved with an innocent trusting love which can possibly only be offered to you by children. One such magic moment came when my little son pushed aside a mop of tousled hair and looked up to see me standing in the doorway. For a moment he seemed to think I was not of this world but just some longed-for dream-person. Then he scrambled to his feet and jumping over heads and legs, anything that might block his path, he flung himself into my arms.

Well, needless to say, that was quite enough for me. There were still some weeks of term to go but he took it for granted that he was leaving immediately and I was only too happy to go along with such a splendid notion. There was only one moment of hesitation when he suddenly remembered something which he had left behind in the gym hall. Cigarettes were scarce in Germany when he had left. He showed me a little tin half-filled with his friends' cigarette stubs which he had been collecting for his father.

Then again there was a chapter so recent that whenever I thought about it, I was uncertain whether I should feel pleased with myself or downright ashamed.

I had not been destined to stay long in Codicote after our arrival: barely a week had passed before news reached me of my favourite uncle, who was also my godfather. Since the death of his wife, my Uncle Cecil had lived alone in a mansion of enormous proportions overlooking Hyde Park, being cared for by an elderly retainer, formerly his butler, known to one and all as Mr Wilkins. The message amounted almost to an SOS telling me, to my dismay, that Mr Wilkins had died quite suddenly when preparing to proceed upstairs with my uncle's early morning cup of tea.

Uncle Cecil had been exceptionally generous to me for as long as I could remember and, on hearing of this, I suggested to his family that I should move in temporarily and try to arrange for new staff to look after him. Needless to say my offer was accepted with alacrity and after some weeks I could well understand why.

Lack of space, at least, was no longer to be a problem, for my uncle's mansion, No. 13 Hyde Park Gardens, could have housed a small army. It was equipped with a huge library, a ballroom, a dining hall, several drawing rooms and, on upper floors, endless lofty bedrooms and bathrooms, while ten or twelve smaller bedrooms on the top floor completed the picture. All floors could be reached by an antiquated lift which was inclined to get stuck now and again and was provided with a strident whistle which, if the occupier got stuck, alerted a member of the household who then had to give one of its gates a mighty kick to start it on its way once again.

I had never actually penetrated the kitchen quarters before arriving to take up my temporary task, but soon learned that finding staff to replace Mr Wilkins looked like becoming the job of a lifetime. We had several answers to our advertisements in the newspapers and I interviewed a number of very suitable candidates who seemed favourably impressed with my uncle's financial intentions, but I could never complete a guided tour of the basement in which they were destined to live before being given to understand that to continue further would be a waste of time. Not surprising really, as I had discovered that the kitchen quarters could only be compared in size with, perhaps, Piccadilly Circus Underground Station. A huge kitchen, quite capable of accommodating a full-sized bowling alley, was ruled over by a kitchen range which I felt would have had no trouble roasting an ox. Innumerable coal houses, sculleries and butler's pantries and three or four large empty cells, which my aunt had used as air-raid shelters, more or less completed the scene.

As the weeks passed, the children's school holidays came and went as did the artless victims I managed to lure into the basement, at most, for a day or so; my temporary stay looked like becoming a permanency.

In some ways our move to London had its brighter side

in that Peter, never very adept at doing nothing, soon met up with an old friend, Werner von Simson, also married to an English girl and, who, after spending some time in an internment camp, was now bent on starting up a small export business. Werner was an asset anyway for besides being extremely astute, he was inclined to eye the goings-on in the world with much amusement; an attitude which I found could very easily become infectious. The centre of what he called his future industrial empire was a tiny office in Birmingham and he was content to overlook the fact that Peter's exit visa did not include a work permit, and to invite him to join in, so long as he could fit inside the door.

For my part I found that by living nearer to the centre of things I could play a more active role in our Memorial Fund, relieving the *Observer* of our presence and establishing our headquarters (consisting of two typewriters and a few cardboard boxes) in one of the many empty upstairs bedrooms. I could also meet more easily with such endlessly helpful friends as David Astor, Isobel Cripps and Victor Gollancz.

As for my uncle, he seemed to enjoy having the boys and the noise about him, and they were happy to have found a brand-new grandfather who studied their stamp collections with assiduous attention and did not seem to mind if they tore around his outsize veranda on their roller-skates. I, too, valued the evenings we spent together reading before the fire in the library or listening to the natural eloquence with which he could describe his career in the House of Commons and now the House of Lords. I realized that only one subject was definitely taboo, for it was then that he could betray a totally unexpected contradiction in an otherwise most equitable character. Quite simply he could not abide Jews. He never mentioned why, although rumour had it that during a period in the Foreign Office, some time long before the First World War, he had had some unpleasing experience with the machinations of certain jewish diamond merchants in South Africa which, he insisted, had been the cause of the outbreak of the Boer War.

* * *

The day arrived when Victor Gollancz and I were lunching together at The Ivy, a favourite haunt of his, and I found him unusually down-hearted. It seemed that for some time he had known that his Trust Fund, 'Save Europe Now', would have to move house, as an unexploded bomb had been discovered underneath their offices in Covent Garden. He had procrastinated but the authorities had now given him three days in which to clear the place and as yet he had found no new accommodation. He had every reason for sadness, for he had many plans, and a devoted staff, and he envisaged the winding-up of a venture which was very close to his heart.

I do not know when it was that the thought of those upstairs bedrooms at No. 13 flashed across my mind, but it was of necessity short-lived. Victor was a Jew and as far as my Uncle Cecil was concerned that would be that.

However, when I returned from the luncheon and stood in the echoing hallway, still thinking of Victor and his dilemma, one of my better ideas occurred to me. At least it seemed so at the time. Need I ask Uncle Cecil after all? Need he in fact know? The more I thought about it the clearer it became and it all seemed so simple.

Three days and the move forced upon him would bring Victor to Saturday, and on Saturdays my uncle retired to his country estate in Egham, returning only on Monday morning. On weekdays the household routine was extremely regular. At 9.00 a.m. the lift must be waiting at the second floor to bring my uncle down to breakfast; and at 7.00 p.m. on the ground floor to transport him upstairs to change for dinner. If Victor's faithful staff could arrive in the basement at 8.00 a.m., even travelling two at a time, they could all be at the top of the house before my uncle appeared and be back home again before the lift had to perform its evening mission.

The plan seemed fairly flawless and on the following weekend my uncle had hardly left for the country before the sound of the lift creaking up and down went on for what seemed a very long time – it could surely not take such ages to transport what I imagined to be a few typewriters. But when evening silence fell, and I travelled up to the attic, to my consternation, I found ten well-equipped offices, chairs, tables, filing cabinets, typewriters – the lot. Victor's faithful staff had achieved a miracle.

There would be no use pretending that I was not relieved when three weeks later a telephone call from Victor told me that all was well, he had found new accommodation and on the following Saturday the caravanserai could move out.

Saturday arrived and with it the appearance at breakfast of my Uncle Cecil holding on to a large white handkerchief. He had a little cold and had decided in the night that he would not leave for the country that day, but would prefer to stay for the weekend in London.

No amount of trying to persuade him that there was really nothing better for a cold than good fresh country air could move him an inch. His mind was made up; and as for fresh air, he might take a little stroll in the park during the day but that would be sufficient.

Two frantic telephone calls, unanswered, convinced me that my well-deserved fate was on its way and that there was little I could do about it beyond seating myself in the library hoping for the best, praying that Victor's exit might be swifter than his entrance or that my uncle might get lost in the park!

Fate was not on my side, for hardly had the heavy front door slammed behind my uncle, setting forth on his little stroll, before the well-remembered rumpus started up in the basement. Up and down – up and down – the lift, thoroughly overtaxed, creaked and groaned, emitting one whistle after another, and I was so busy wishing I had never been born that I did not notice the door to the library opening quietly until I looked up to see my uncle, still in hat, gloves and woolly scarf, standing in the doorway.

There was a slight pause and then – 'Chrismary,' he said (as a child I was always called Chrismary by the family in order to differentiate me from my mother). 'On returning from my walk a little earlier than usual, there being a mischievous nip in the air, I came across a large furniture van parked outside and some unusual-looking individuals – possibly Balkan terrorists – who seemed to be emptying my house of furniture. Would you have any idea what is afoot?'

Had I any idea? At that moment I could think of only one, which was to spill the beans, to mention his dislike of Jews, to tell him of Victor's plight and to confess to my own efforts at trying to deal with my conscience when it came to Victor's race. I was listened to in silence, only being interrupted once to be asked just how long had he entertained the uninvited guests.

'Three weeks?'

He made the words sound like three centuries and then added, 'Dear me, what an intolerable situation.'

To which I could only answer meekly that I quite agreed – intolerable.

After my narrative petered out there were several minutes of complete silence when I found myself examining the faded carpet about me with exaggerated intensity. Then Uncle Cecil rose to his feet and made for the door, but before leaving the library he turned and cleared his throat. Now I was in for it – I braced myself for the onslaught – but no!—

'Chrismary,' he said, 'at this moment I can think of nothing whatsoever to say, but may I make myself quite clear – let it never happen again.' Yes, indeed, just as much as I loved him I think my Uncle Cecil must have loved me – and he showed his love when a telephone call from Werner, closely followed by a visit from two policemen, arrived to tell me of the accident. I must leave for Birmingham immediately, he would see that Christopher was brought from his kindergarten and delivered to my sister safe and sound. Had I money? Taxis, train tickets, everything must be done to bring me soonest to Peter's bedside.

So my vigil had started and as the hours passed and darkness became dawn I learned how easy it is for thoughts to turn into fantasies.

A caring, soft-voiced Irish night nurse brought me cups of tea and took my place occasionally. She came from Connemara and she was homesick and we could talk together in whispers of her home on that far western coast. What had the surgeon in mind when he talked of recovery? If he awoke – no, *when* he awoke – would Peter ever be able to go back to a post-war rat race?

Many years ago, with Hitler heading for war, Peter and I had talked of Ireland and of farming there perhaps. At the time it was not to be, but now? Surely just fantasy, but the smell of those turf fires, the sound of the sea and of the wind blowing over heather-covered hills, sometimes allowed that little nurse and I to leave the ache of homesickness and the sorrow of separation behind us and carry us away together to a dream world all of our own.

At 5 o'clock in the morning of the seventh day Peter returned from his other world and opened his eyes. For a short while, he looked about at the walls, the ceiling, seemingly unsurprised at the strangeness of his surroundings and when he saw me sitting there he simply asked, 'Where have you been?' and added, 'I've been looking for you all over the place.' And I heard my voice answering, 'I don't really know where I've been, all over the place too I guess,' which, when I come to think of it, was not far from the truth.

PART TWO

Ireland

'The history of a nation is not in parliaments and battlefields, but in what the people say to each other on fair days and high days and in how they farm and quarrel and go on pilgrimage'

W. B. YEATS

Chapter Nine

WAIT TILL I tell you! One does not have to live long in Ireland before recognizing that by accepting such an invitation to move in closer by the fireside, at the crossroads, indeed, anywhere you happen to be at the time, you are in for much enjoyment. For whether the tale you are about to listen to be tragic, hilarious or plain dubious, you can be assured of melodrama. 'Whisht on you! Mary, Mother of God, could you believe it? Honest to God, don't be talking!': such are the enthusiastic interjections which help to urge things along to the inevitable climax. It could be a marriage — 'a grand poor fellow, but herself, thanks-be, with a plot of land'; or a funeral — 'no Will, God rest his soul, and couldn't you slate the roof with the uncles and cousins that turned up from across the water for the wake'. Perhaps, even a law case, but surely best of all a possible scandal, with the parish priest giving-out fit to deafen the saints.

If I were to begin my own particular story, as again all Irish sagas mostly do, hidden somewhere in the mists of time, I would have to go back to the year of our Lord 1610 when two brothers, the younger sons of yeoman farmers from Shropshire in England, left their homeland

and set sail for Ireland, choosing to settle in a far western corner of that turbulent island. Their names were Francis and Thomas Burton and it was not too difficult to discover their reason for choosing County Clare to be their future home.

At the end of the sixteenth century, when Clare was a kingdom, the O'Briens, most powerful of the clans, decided (with only the occasional back-slide) to link their fortunes with those of the English Crown. Their allegiance did them no harm, for their chieftain at the time was created Earl of Thomond and, unlike others within the new county, their lands were not confiscated. Instead they were rewarded with added acres to their already large possessions. Indeed, in 1610 Donagh O'Brien, fourth Earl of Thomond, together with his brother, Daniel, Baron Inchiquin, doubtless in order to clinch matters, became Protestant converts and their lands stretched from Bunratty in the east of the county to Carrigaholt in the far south-west.

The West of Ireland had not yet been stripped of her famous Irish oak forests in order to build the English fleet, and, according to records of the time, you could travel the O'Brien lands, from one corner to the other, without seeing the sky.

I could believe that no lands, no fortified castles were secure in those days when other mighty clans like the O'Neills and the O'Donnells were ever ready to descend in their hordes, in the respectable cause of Irish freedom and independence, ravaging and plundering the countryside before returning to their northern fastnesses loaded with useful booty. It thus makes sense that in 1610 the O'Briens, Lords of Thomond, were only too happy to welcome as tenant settlers reliable fellow Protestants of sturdy English yeoman stock who could assist them in warding off such damaging forays.

It is said that Ireland has the ability to absorb her conquerors, so that those who would wish to impose their will, to alter a way of life which has survived the centuries, soon give up the hopeless task and settle down to become more Irish than the Irish themselves. But for those who leave her shores, there are always the dreams of *Tír na nÓg*, the golden land of eternal youth, or of *Tuath de Danaan*, the little people or the Banshee wail heralding approaching death. These myths lurking in the misty hedgerows, drifting wraith-like about the rounded summits of her ancient hills are siren songs which never allow them to forget the land from whence they came.

When I returned to live in Ireland, 337 years later, I had little knowledge and not much interest in my Anglo-Irish ancestry. Nor do I think that my attachment came from some inborn mythical urge, but rather that, having been brought up in England in a very orderly household, where meals appeared on the dot and bedtime was bedtime, and then in Germany where *Ordnung* was a compulsory fact of life, the Ireland of my memories was of joyous journeyings to a land where nothing whatsoever functioned as I had learned that it should.

My upbringing, for instance, had included a very liberal attitude towards religion, particularly when it came to church-going, but I only had to cross the Irish Sea to discover that religion played a serious role in the lives of my Irish relatives, all active supporters of their church – the Protestant Church of Ireland. Their loyalty was influenced a little, perhaps, by having to compare their small, isolated battalions, their elderly weather-beaten houses of prayer, with the colourful armies of 'Holy Romans' who poured forth every Sunday from their newly built, highly varnished, monoliths of cold grey stone.

The battle was an uneven one, but my Irish relatives did not falter, keeping up a useful rear-guard action with garden fêtes and sales of work, when home-made jams, books and discarded clothing, tinker tents and hoopla stands all contributed to keeping the roof intact and the old organ blowing in the church of their ancestors.

'Putting up a show, keeping up the side', these I could remember were expressions often used to underline the necessity for donning our Sunday best, swallowing our breakfasts and grabbing our hymn books, preparatory to joining the

119

select band of local 'Prods' in the seldom very melodious worship of our God.

But, although in many ways hide-bound, steadfastly refusing to recognize that their role in Irish history had suffered a body blow with the founding of the Irish Free State, and still talking doggedly of Sackville Street, Queenstown, King's County and so on, they had also refused to abandon a happy capacity to look upon unorthodox behaviour as being quite normal and acceptable.

There was, for instance, my Uncle Ned, who was firmly convinced that no worthwhile roof had been constructed in Ireland since the end of the eighteenth century. The slates came then from Bangor in Wales, he explained, and the craftsmen in those days were artisans who had gone out with the dodo. He was considered rather mad later, as he carried this conviction a little too far, refusing to have his roof repaired when leaks appeared and finally ending his days sleeping under an umbrella in the dining-room. But I did not find him mad when as a child I sat with him on the banks of the Slaney and watched him pick out a suitable fly from his old tweed hat and cast it with unerring exactitude over the still pool of waters below. Nor when he led me by the hand through the jungle of his walled gardens to that distant corner where he tended his prize roses. He never got around to cultivating a particular rose which he had promised to name after me, but he always assured me that he had it in mind.

Then there was my cousin's wedding. I will call her Cousin Letitia and, at thirty-nine years of age, she seemed to me at the time a very elderly lady. There was, of course, general rejoicing when at last she got her man, for although he was no film star, whatever was missing so far as physical charm was concerned was made up for by the fact that he was gentry and owned two hundred acres of prime grazing land in County Meath.

In order to celebrate in a manner suited to the occasion a domestic hire service had been approached and a butler engaged to take command of the household staff, which normally consisted of two pretty little girls from the village, each aged about fourteen.

As is usual in Ireland, things were soon running late. The Reverend Canon, a relative of the bridegroom who had come over from England to conduct the wedding service, had somehow been unable to wind up his sermon, and afterwards those of the guests who had motor cars found themselves unable to start their engines. Nonetheless, late or no, as the guests finally made it to the bride's home, the noble presence of the hired butler certainly added an air of glamour to the proceedings, particularly as he and the little girls had obviously busied themselves filling every vase, bowl and bucket they could find with flowers, and spreading out the wedding presents most tastefully in the dining-room. Unfortunately, not quite so obviously, at least at the start, the butler had also spent some of the time at his disposal in opening bottles and sampling the champagne. I do not know when it was that he decided that the guests, Mr and Mrs So-and-So, the Reverend and Mrs Whats-it, were not really up to his usual standard and proceeded to add the odd title here and there. Anglo-Irish gentry are rather fond of titles but when Lieutenants and Captains became Colonels and even Generals, and anyone wearing a clerical collar was assured of at least a bishopric, it had to be acknowledged that something was amiss. The climax was reached when the butler, now well into his stride, cast caution to the winds and in stentorian tones announced, 'The Lord and Lady Inglenook'. The local auctioneer who then slipped in with his wife did not allow himself to look anything more than slightly surprised when so suddenly raised to the peerage, but his wife got a fit of the giggles which lasted for the rest of the afternoon.

If this had happened in England, a severe reprimand at least would have ensued. As for Germany, dear me! there would almost have been a revolution, certainly a law case, and the chorus of, 'Unerhört' and, 'Mein Gott, was soll das?' would have spoiled the festivities altogether. Instead I do not remember hearing one word of startled surprise, let alone of condemnation. On the contrary, as we pushed the bridal couple up the drive in their newly furbished Morris Minor, it was generally agreed that the wedding had been a splendid affair altogether.

Finally, already in my teens, I would stay with my close friend, Gwennie McCormack, at Moore Abbey, her home in County Kildare, and in the evenings we would gather around the piano in the drawing-room where her father, the world-renowned tenor, John McCormack, allowed us to sing with him – opera, *lieder* and haunting Irish melodies – which reduced us all, including himself, to tears. They were magical evenings which gave me the courage to become a singer myself, although Gwennie and I, when sharing a bedroom at night and able to have interminable discussions as to our futures, were both agreed that we would, of course, also get married one day. Seeing that she was spending her school days in a convent where she was not allowed to take a bath without donning a pair of black combinations, and I in an establishment where prowess on the lacrosse field was considered far more important than an awareness of life, it was not surprising that our conception of the married state never got much further than picturing ourselves duly veiled, in gorgeous white dresses, being swept down the aisle by an Adonis whom we had promised to look after for the rest of our lives.

After Peter's accident I was faced with realities. Selly Oak Hospital insisted that, if released from the casualty ward, he would have to spend at least seven more weeks in hospital in care and under surveillance. But this did not coincide with Peter's own opinion as to his future. Two weeks later, when I was hardly back in London, a telephone call from the surgeon told me that he was up and rampaging about the place, threatening to leave in his pyjamas if they did not return his clothes. 'He is still a very ill man, Mrs Bielenberg, and he needs medical care,' the surgeon told me, 'but we are not a prison and I will have to ask you to take him home.'

Whenever I read in the newspaper that people who are

institutionalized would be far better off if cared for at home, I think of those weeks of Peter's convalescence and, to be honest, my sympathy lies with the home.

The following months were surely no easier for Peter than for anyone else trying to behave as if everything was as normal as before. We sympathized, tried to tread carefully, to bypass the ever-recurring monologues on the theme of his having to return forthwith to Germany where he was needed, and to overlook his explosions of helpless frustration when he found that he could not cross a London street without breaking out in a cold sweat. The surgeon had been correct of course about the state of his health and, although seemingly unable to do anything right, I listened and tried to produce words of encouragement, at the same time aware that the thought of returning to Germany was for me becoming an ever-increasing anathema. Worst of all, I could not ignore a creeping sensation that someone I loved and who had shared my life had suddenly become a stranger. It was not to be long before an occasional glance in the mirror was enough to let me know that Peter was not the only one who was looking the worse for wear.

It was when I had got as far as wondering whether all this might mean a parting of the ways, that my mother, in her own practical fashion, stepped into the breach.

Fresh country air being, in her opinion, a certain cure for all ills, both physical and psychic, and with Uncle Cecil, at least, temporarily catered for by a family of amateur retainers who seemed content in the cellars, we were back in Codicote, ensconced in her experimental house at the far end of the vegetable garden. She had grown very fond of Peter, admiring his energy and sharing with him a certain direct way of expressing an opinion; in simple terms, she usually called a spade a spade. An active person herself, she could also understand his frustration, although fully aware that he was not what she called, 'his usual self'. Something similar had happened to my father after being shell-shocked in the First World War – 'difficult, dear, a little difficult' – but he had recovered as would Peter and she did not approve of giving in when things became a 'little difficult'.

Although Germany must be a dreadful place, she could well understand his wanting to get back there and his not being happy in England, where Germans as a whole were not exactly popular just at present, and particularly when he had nothing to do now beyond wondering about his future health. To uproot the children all over again would be nonsense, as would be parting company. Some compromise must be found. Peter had once confided to her that one of his dreams as a boy had been to become a farmer and, before the war, when it looked as if Hitler had come to stay and war was imminent, had we not had some plan to leave for Ireland?

I knew that she herself felt no particular attachment to Ireland, viewing the scene there with, at best, amused incomprehension. Her orderly mind was not easily able to understand the rather haphazard lifestyle of my Irish relatives; as for the social conditions prevailing, 'Too many prelates for me, dear – far too many.'

But now, although she was not certain of having found a solution, dithering was not a solution either, so maybe it was worth giving it a try. She ended her little speech in very typical manner, by advising me to go over to Ireland first with the children; the summer holidays were upon us and these would probably drive Peter even further up the wall. 'Make up your mind, dear. I have lots of plans for the garden which will keep Peter busy for a few weeks. If you want my advice, do it now.'

So, in the summer of 1947, the children and I set off by train for the Fishguard Ferry in Wales, bound for Rosslare in County Wexford and for Kilmore Quay, a fishing village some fourteen miles down the coast to the south-west, where a guest house had been highly recommended by several Irish relatives. Although the journey ahead of us was to be long and tedious, as soon as we arrived on the platform at Paddington Station I was immediately made aware, as in years gone by, that I had left England behind me and was surrounded by boisterous foreigners. Young men, old men, family parties, children galore, cloth caps worn over one eye, bulging sacks and cardboard suitcases only prevented from bursting apart by bits of old rope. These were the exiles returning home for a bit of a holiday after helping England to conquer the enemy in their own way.

When it finally drew in to the platform the train was filthy. It was as if the authorities were determined to ensure that this journey to their homeland should be made as unattractive as possible for the Irish. As we crowded on board though, my fellow passengers were in no mood to show resentment. Assorted possessions were soon stacked perilously on the luggage rack and overflowed into the corridors, and the train had hardly gathered speed before a number of bottles appeared from nowhere and started doing the rounds. What will it be? Would I care for a jar? Irish voices are particularly gentle and pleasant; Irish manners likewise, and although I was the only female in the compartment it would have been unmannerly to leave me out. For my part I remembered enough about Irish drinking etiquette to refuse. I had no alcohol with me and could therefore not manage 'my round' should it come to my turn to provide. 'A mineral, then, for the lads?' Their generosity knew no bounds, and as the train rattled along through the night, and the children were finally asleep on the floor, I closed my eyes, trying to doze off, but finding myself listening to the ceaseless chatter, drifting in and out of a different world from the one I had been accustomed to in Ireland. This one was not that of the happy-go-lucky, come-down-in-the-world Anglo-Irish gentry, but one in which the Mammy and the Da played an almost exaggerated role, where funerals were 'luvly' and teeth a nuisance. I sensed that a certain amount of showing off would be the order of the day, when these returning heroes arrived at the family hearth. For they had seen the world, Manchester, Birmingham, Coventry, one had fought 'them Germans' and all had been in air raids. Another had even risked breaking a rigid law of his country and ventured inside a Protestant church – a funeral to be sure, but what a funeral, beautiful altogether, the music, the flowers – 'Jaysus, I am telling you, we are not buried at all over here' was a conclusion seemingly shared by all.

I must have slept for a little for when I awakened the bottles were empty and the sounds reverberating around the carriage were similar to those inclined to erupt when the pubs close in Kilburn. What England had done to them and what they were going to do in return was nobody's business. A poor young man called Kevin Barry was hanged from a gallows tree over and over again and the grey dawn never stopped breaking over Kathleen Mavourneen. As for Mother Macree, whatever happened to her became lost in dirge-like dronings and the occasional snore long before we got to Fishguard.

There, to my pleasant surprise, drawn up at the quay, awaiting the arrival of our train, was none other than an old friend, *SS Princess Maud*. It had always been of interest when travelling to Ireland to find out which boat had been laid on for the often stormy crossing of the Irish Sea. If it were 'the Princess', as she was fondly known to her crew, or simply 'the Maud' for those whose politics could not allow a hint of royal connection to cross their lips, one thing was certain: if the surface of the Irish Sea differed only slightly from plate-glass, *SS Princess Maud* behaved in a manner one could only describe as skittish. She had a certain corkscrew movement aft, almost a habit of kicking up her legs behind, which was guaranteed to send the most sea-worthy passengers reaching blindly for the paper bags which were supplied in abundance, or for those who had given up and merely wished to die, to heave up another basinful and really no longer care where it landed.

A further hazard when travelling aboard 'the Princess' was due to her advanced age. Launched decades ago before the First World War, she had battled her way back and forth across the Irish Sea so often that no one could object to her taking her time about it and allowing her, in spite of German submarines and possible torpedoes, to arrive the odd hour or so late. If the day were a weekday and her destination Rosslare Harbour, she docked at the end of a long sea wall which did duty as a pier. Here a small train would wait for her passengers to disembark and transport them to Wexford from whence they could travel on to Dublin or Cork City. If it were a Sunday though, or indeed a Holy Day, this was not always the case. Then the late arrival of the boat might mean that the engine driver would miss morning Mass in Wexford some ten miles up the track; a matter not so much of concern to his job, but to that of his ultimate salvation. On such occasions, therefore, he was wont to depart taking his train with him, leaving late arrivals to a long wait behind inadequate wind shelters or to what was known as 'chancing it'. To chance it, which I remembered to be a very Irish concept, meant lugging one's baggage along a rickety structure composed of planks and bits of rope attached to the windward side of the sea wall.

When, after some years of use this whole contraption collapsed into the sea one stormy night I imagine that the Rosslare Port Authorities were much relieved that it had not done so when loaded with 'chancers' on a Sunday or a Holy Day.

On arrival, I was delighted to find the *Princess Maud* unchanged – the gleaming brass fittings, the red plush bunks, the polished mahogany and even the stewardesses no longer in their first youth, with gentle friendly faces and starched white aprons, waiting to welcome the passengers aboard, as if it were to their own home. The sea was to be only slight and, if I was not mistaken, there would still be that corner of the deck where we could stow ourselves away and avoid the unhappy drama which might soon unfold in the lounges and lavatories below.

My special corner was luckily unoccupied, so that before the Fishguard Harbour lights had faded into the darkness behind us, the children, well wrapped up in rugs, were nearly asleep again. I was unable to sleep but sat there with thoughts already travelling far ahead to a land that I had not seen for more than fifteen years. Would Ireland have changed as I had changed? I was married now and had three sons, and as for Ireland, she had not been at war, but remained a peaceful oasis with nothing much to complain about except the scarcity of tea. She had remained neutral, playing her cards adroitly – sometimes too adroitly for my taste, as when Prime Minister de Valera joined with the German ambassador in a telegram of condolence to the German people on the death of Adolf Hitler. I also had to remember those dubious individuals calling themselves Irish, and carefully to be avoided in Berlin, who were known to be lurking in the corridors of Hitler's Ministry of Propaganda. What were they doing there? They had faded into obscurity as soon as the war was over, but I was older now, more wary perhaps.

The Princess docked punctually at 7 a.m. and sure enough there was the little train, also unchanged, awaiting us at the end of the pier in order to travel some two hundred and fifty yards to Rosslare Harbour Station, where we hoped to be met by motor car. Before departing on this little trip, the guard went from carriage door to carriage door locking it firmly on the outside. I remembered once as a schoolgirl travelling alone, asking the guard why. 'To stop the folk from flying out of the window, me darlin'' had been his explanation, which was, I suppose, as good a reason as any.

The journey accomplished and the carriage doors unlocked, I stood on the harbour platform looking about me. The coastguards' cottages up on the cliff, the rusty old dredger in the bay, the fishing boats, the sea gulls, the soft morning air; nothing had changed, except that the little stone-built waiting-room was sporting a new title and the adjoining public conveniences likewise. No longer 'Ladies' and 'Gents', they were now '*Fir*' and '*Mna*' and here some confusion was already taking place as those not up to date with the Gaelic revival and uncertain whether they were '*Fir*' or '*Mna*' dodged in and swiftly out again having opted for the wrong one.

We had not long to wait before we were met by an extremely pleasant little man who introduced himself as Mick and who led us to the shell of a spacious motor car parked on the hill leading down to the harbour. A large piece of rock wedged under one of the front wheels had to be removed, the vehicle started to roll and the engine sprang into life just in time to prevent us hitting the harbour wall. We stopped twice before reaching Kilmore Quay, once to collect a newspaper and again to load up a large crate of Guinness which Mick explained was for a fellow guest who was in the position of not being able to do without it.

The guesthouse in Kilmore proved something of a surprise. It was situated at the far end of the village, overlooking the sea and consisted of a ramshackle bungalow, two caravans propped up rather perilously on some logs of wood and what looked like a converted hen-house. The hen-house was called the annexe and had been prepared for the children. The owner of the guesthouse, a Mrs Godfrey, greeted us in the doorway. She proved to be a lady of ample proportions, so ample in fact, as I learned later, that she had had to relinquish her role as Master of Hounds when she became too heavy for her horse. But I learned immediately that her voice had lost none of the carrying power usually associated with the hunting field for, on seeing us and before bidding us welcome, she bellowed into the darkness of the hallway behind her, where I suppose fellow guests had been discussing the implications of a name like Bielenberg, 'They are not Jews!'.

Mick, too, was somewhat out of the ordinary, acting not only as the establishment's chauffeur, but also as the gardener, the house maid, the parlour maid and the kitchen maid, although his main interest seemed to be his role as Honorary Secretary to the Life Boat Association.

At that time Britons in their hundreds were crossing the Irish Sea in order to escape for a week or so the conditions brought about by having won the war. The Wexford Chamber of Commerce decided that something must be done to exploit such a favourable opportunity. Bacon and eggs, soda bread, country butter, fish from the rivers and lobster from the sea were not, it seemed, enough to attract the more fastidious tourist, especially Americans, whose sole interest seemed to centre upon their Irish origins and the plumbing. The Chamber issued a decree, therefore, that each little house aspiring to accommodate paying guests must be possessed of a bath-tub and an indoor lavatory. This ruling presented

Kilmore with quite a problem. For though several cottages had applied for a licence to be registered, the only bath-tub for miles around was owned by Mrs Godfrey. I had, at first, been somewhat nonplussed to discover that this tub, which was of noble proportions with big shining taps and splendid drainage fittings, was not attached to any water supply. The reason for this became clear when the postman reported the imminent arrival of an inspector from Wexford who was doing the rounds to discover if those who had applied for a tourist licence had also complied with the ruling as to the plumbing.

On hearing this news the entire village moved into gear with spontaneous alacrity. Mrs Godfrey's, of course, must be his first visit where tea and hot scones and the bath-tub would await him. It was then for Mick to lead him off around the corner to the Life Boat House, considered to be another very potent tourist attraction. They were barely inside the building and I could imagine Mick waxing lyrical on the subject of his beloved life boat when a tractor and trailer appeared from nowhere. It drew up behind the hen-house and four sturdy young men moved quietly into the house and headed for the bathroom. In a matter of minutes the bath was out of the back door, through the gate, on to the trailer and away! It had four further visits to make and I could only imagine that either the inspector had been born in the district and joined in the game, or else something a good deal stronger than tea and scones was provided for his refreshment *en route*.

In the evening of that day, when the cortège returned, I was leaning over the sea-wall staring out towards the Saltee Islands and the sunset, listening to the familiar sea sounds of small waves lapping against the rocks and of boats chugging off to the fishing grounds with their retinue of clamouring sea gulls.

The tractor, the trailer, Mick and the bath had been joined by quite a few happy hangers-on and Mick assured me that all had gone well. The inspector had been a grand poor fellow altogether and before he had left had even given him a couple of shillings for the Life Boat.

I think it was then I came to a final decision. I knew that it was far too soon to think in finalities, that there were still too many obstacles along the path, but I seemed to have found a goal I must strive for. I must return to live in this strange haphazard country, return and live out my days. There had been too much organization in my life so far, too much authority. Beautiful bath-tub, beautiful Kilmore, beautiful Ireland, could it be that I had found a corner of the world where those other outlandish concepts could never hope to survive?

On our return to England, it was a joy to discover that Peter's health had greatly improved. My mother's brand of 'care and surveillance' had obviously been far more successful than mine. To look after him she had engaged a daily lady whose interest in politics did not extend beyond the village, and whose Hertfordshire accent he could barely understand anyway. To remedy inactivity she had 'started him off' in the vegetable garden which he had transformed from a rough field into a chessboard of symmetrical exactitude.

So far so good, but in spite of Peter's return to comparative health, as the months passed and 1947 became 1948, there still seemed no glimmer of permanency in our lives. The path seemed to wind on ahead of us, but a sense of direction was missing. I do not, therefore, find it easy to pin-point any one particular event, any loosely shaped plan which might have influenced our progress one way or another.

It could have been when news reached us that Peter's mother was suffering from hunger oedema and, with the help of Lord Pakenham who now headed the British Control Commission in Germany, we could obtain a special visa for her to come and see us in England. She had sacrificed her health for her grandchildren and if we had any illusions as to the seriousness of the food situation in Germany we could learn from her at first hand of the conditions still prevailing there.

It could have been that, as travel regulations between Germany and England were eased and Peter could travel back to Frankfurt to learn that, belonging as he did to a missing generation, he need have no fear of not getting prestigious employment. But on this same journey he met Marion Dönhoff who, although involved with her newspaper, was lonely in Hamburg and still dreamed of wide open spaces, of those lost estates in East Prussia which had been in her family for hundreds of years. If we could collect visas for Ireland, or even Canada, for her scattered family and two good friends who were also expert in land management, why not pool our resources, form a co-operative, get back to the land, start life anew? Together they filled the air with new possibilities and doubtless added to Peter's own indecision. For I suppose that I, too, must have been hovering in the background. The *Observer* seemingly still had use for my services and I had been back and forth to Germany several times, privileged in being allowed to assist (which really meant learn from) their permanent correspondent – Sebastian Haffner, to my mind one of the great journalists of his day.

Maybe my sense of alienation which increased with each visit came about because I was in uniform and in some ways was cut off from the daily round. It had to be different for Peter. Germany was his country. I had tried it before and had been happy there, able to identify with so many others whose friendship I valued and whose ideals I could share. But Germany had simply slaughtered them and, for me, it was just like any country vigorously trying to forget the past and to concentrate on establishing a respectable, above all prosperous, future for itself. Somehow I could not contemplate trying to live there again.

I am inclined to agree with those who consider that an English upbringing which enjoins bottling up the emotions and adopting a stiff upper lip when facing adversity is an uncomfortable fallacy. My Italian sister-in-law, who could bawl her head off for a few minutes and then double-up with laughter, at least had it easier.

Psycho-somatism was an unknown concept to me in those days, although I had certainly experienced times when emotional upheaval sparked off acute physical pain; for instance, in Berlin, when I had felt obliged to tell a young Jewish couple that I could not harbour them in our house for longer than a few days[1] or when I had heard of Peter's accident and was standing by his bedside in that Birmingham hospital. Now though, as 1948 moved into place, pain rather than being sporadic became constant and my health broke down completely.

I was sent off to Harley Street where various medical pundits looked extremely concerned and told me that I would have to have an operation. In fact they voiced their combined opinions in such doom-laden obscurity that they succeeded in putting the fear of God into me and I thought it wise to take a leaf in practical behaviour from my mother's book and make my Will. They also told me I needed 'building up' before they could take to their knives, and suggested Eastbourne as a possible venue. Eastbourne? Where the hell was Eastbourne? Peter was now in charge. He knew of my love for the mountains and, before I realized what exactly was afoot, he had alerted a very good Swiss friend who was only too happy to send us official invitations and whisked me off to Switzerland, where after a fortnight of sun and snow the pundits, this time Swiss pundits, decided to do the deed. They removed my gall bladder and my Will could be relegated to the waste-paper basket.

I have recorded certain details of those months of indecision when it seemed to me that as a family we had become little more than privileged gypsies. It was a time when I had to hope that, while their parents were trying to sort out their lives, our three sons, although never certain as to where they would be spending their next school holidays, were doing

1 See *The Past is Myself*.

likewise. The auspices seemed favourable: Nicky was soon to become Head Boy at Dane Court; Johnny was resigned to it, in spite of writing home that he now knew why it was called 'boring' school; and Christopher, in Bexhill-on-Sea at a little school recommended by a friend and approved of by her small daughter, was having his nails scrubbed, his teeth cleaned and his hair trimmed in office-boy style, none of which seemed to upset him unduly.

And I can record that Peter and I rode out these storms together, side by side, and finally arrived at the moment on 28th August 1948 which brought him on his first visit to Ireland. To be exact the moment when, once more astride his ancient motor cycle, he arrived before the door of an aunt of mine who lived near Athy in County Kildare.

Chapter Ten

I SUPPOSE IT all really started when a lump of turf fell out of the fire in the sitting-room and burned a large hole in my aunt's hearthrug. The rug had surely seen better days, but after all she was insured and here was a chance to get a new one. My aunt had quite a reputation for making insurance claims, but usually got away with it because she was also most useful in getting new clients for the Insurance Company. So it was that the insurance agent, who was obviously a frequent visitor, turned up promptly to assess the damage. He was in a hurry that day though, for he had a difficult task ahead of him. One of his clients, who had failed to pay his bill for two years, had told him of his continued inability to pay in cash, but of his willingness to give him a horse instead. The agent had closed the deal before he had been given to understand that the horse was not waiting patiently to be collected from its stable, but had broken out some days before and had been seen contentedly grazing some bogland about ten miles away. The agent was nothing if not resourceful, and rather than lose a client he had borrowed a horse-box, hitched it to his motor car and set out to catch the horse before nightfall.

Here I must digress in order to describe another of my aunt's paying guests, and, to keep the record straight, declare that he was not the only one of his ilk helping to keep the wolf from the door in bleak mansions throughout Ireland. In my aunt's case, this important source of income came from a retired army officer who had succumbed to the bottle and whose relatives were willing to pay handsomely in order to keep him out of England. In former days he had risen to the rank of major in a prestigious British cavalry regiment and was known to the rest of the household as 'The Mage'. When he was sober, no one could have been more amiable, nor more polished, radiating that kind of honourable innocence often displayed by those who choose the Army for a career. When he was drunk there was no holding him. A short visit to a public house, of which there were many in the local town, a rapid downing of several outsize gins, and he would explode onto the pavement singing and dancing and ready to fling himself about the neck of any female who happened to get in his way. The Irish are adept at dealing with such situations, but after complaints arrived from the convent that when in this state he had shown himself unable to discriminate between ordinary housewives doing their bit of shopping and those who had taken the veil, my aunt's main concern was to keep him as near to her side as possible, whereas that of the Mage, of course, was to discover ways and means of evading her watchful eye.

Now at the mention of the word horse the ex-cavalry officer became very attentive, and from the glint in his eye I could tell that he was busy making several important calculations. 'See here, dear boy,' he said to the agent as smoothly as could be, 'this is where I can be of help. Dammit, I've lived with horses all my life. It's not that easy to catch a horse. Take me along with you and you'll need no horse-box. I'll catch the nag for you and ride it back here and we can put it up in the stable until you can sell it. What about that for a solution?'

The agent, who for diplomatic reasons had been kept in ignorance of the Mage's occasional escapades, looked highly relieved. 'Thank you, sir,' he said. 'In fact thanks a million, that is indeed an idea.' And the words were hardly out of his mouth before the Mage had nipped upstairs and returned, all spit and polish in riding boots and breeches.

My aunt was known in the district to be an ingenious character, but also one who could recognize a dilemma when it came her way. Now she knew herself to be in a fix, for nothing but trouble could arise if the Mage were let loose in the district – even if he were on horseback. On the other hand, the insurance money for the mat in the sitting-room had not yet reached the bank account and there was always that rusty ballcock in the water tank upstairs. If that got stuck again – as she often hoped it would – the staircase and the hallway would soon be awash, and they had needed redecorating for a long time. She decided to plump for letting the Mage go, hoping for the best, and at the same time asking Peter and my cousin please to go along on the expedition and to try their best to keep things in some sort of order.

Some three hours later they returned; at least Peter, the insurance agent and my cousin did so. They were very pleased with themselves and reported that the outing had been a complete success. They had taken some time to locate the whereabouts of the horse, but once having done so, the Mage had taken over with true professionalism, approaching it with care, coaxing and calling, and finally slipping a halter over its head with the greatest of ease.

But where was the Mage right now? Well, that was rather difficult to say. The last they had seen of him he was cantering along beside the road, an upright military presence heading purposefully for the next village. 'A grand man altogether,' declared the insurance agent in his innocence, and we sat down to wait for news of what we felt must be certain disaster.

It was now that Peter started talking to the insurance agent. We were in deep trouble. Our grand ideas of forming a co-operative with the Dönhoffs had fallen through. Marion had become increasingly involved in her newspaper and the others had decided to stay in Germany, all of them having found excellent farming jobs in the Bundesrepublik. Although I sometimes secretly worried about having been too pigheaded about returning to Germany, we had settled on trying to make a go of it on our own in Ireland. We had followed up every advertisement, scouring the countryside for weeks looking for a suitable farm to be purchased at a price we could afford. We had in fact very little capital at our disposal, £5,000 to be exact, and Peter, who spent much of his time studying a series of little volumes called *Teach Yourself Farming*, had assured himself that it was useless to spend every bean on buying the land as we would need more capital to equip and stock it.

I was not making things easier, for after trudging for miles looking for acres he considered workable, he would find me sitting on the motor cycle, a grumpy heap, declaring that I would not be seen dead in the horrible shack which went with them. On the other hand, if I found the house of my dreams, not too big, Georgian, Regency perhaps, with rooms of such happy proportions that I could visualize just how things would look when I moved in with an army of painters and decorators, I could be sure of hearing that the estate, described by the auctioneer in such glowing terms as the best of farming land, was mainly scrub or bog and utterly useless.

That evening the insurance agent listened sympathetically to our tale of woe, nodding his head, while keeping one ear cocked towards the window in the hope that the clatter of horse's hooves would herald the arrival of the Mage.

He seemed hardly to hear when Peter mentioned that he must cover quite a lot of country in the course of his business. Had he not even heard of a place? Could he not perhaps . . .? No, not really, he could not think of anything for the moment – oh, well, but wait, he'd been over in a place called Tullow last week – had some business with an auctioneer over there, one Paddy Dawson, to his way of thinking one of the few honest auctioneers in the whole country, and he had told him of some place he'd been trying to sell for years. Up in the hills; it sounded a desperate sort of a place but he understood from Paddy that it would be going cheap.

A welcome commotion from the yard did not allow him to continue. It turned out to be a neighbouring farmer leading the horse and delivering the Mage, who was fast asleep in his ass-cart. But when the horse was safely bedded down in the stable, the Mage packed off to bed, and the insurance agent had departed with much gratitude, Peter and I sat down before a dying fire and took out our dog-eared old map so liberally spattered over with little red circles to remind us of the many 'gentleman's residences', the hundreds of derelict acres we had inspected with so much hope and left behind us with so much disappointment. Tullow, where was Tullow? Ah no, it was miles away: Athy, Carlow, Tullow; and our ration of petrol was nearing its end, and anyway the motor cycle had got to the stage when it had a puncture almost every day. It was sure to be another dud, just another waste of time and money. It was no use; perhaps farming was a silly idea anyway; perhaps we should have risked it and gone to Canada; perhaps I should not have been so stubborn in my attitude to post-war Germany.

It was then I truly believe that fate came to the conclusion that we had had enough and decided to take a hand in the game, for on the following morning my aunt returned from her shopping trip to town waving the local newspaper and telling us she had made up her mind. Made up her mind, that is, to sell every hen she had in the barnyard.

We had often wondered why she had not come to this decision before, as her birds seemed to suffer from a complete dearth of feathers. This we were led to understand came from the fact that they had developed a disease called 'the Pick' or 'the Peck' which drove them to go at each other hammer and tongs until they all ended up stark naked. It also seemed to inhibit them from laying a single egg.

Now, as a result of reading one of the smaller advertisements in the local newspaper, my aunt had decided on a change. She explained that all her life she had wanted to own Ancona hens, a rare breed; 'little dotes of birds', even their legs were covered with feathers, and now if there wasn't a woman from Newtownbarry who had twelve such birds for sale and they would go fast, so she intended to set off that very day in order to clinch the deal.

139

To set off for Newtownbarry that very day, a distance of at least thirty miles there and thirty miles back, was an almost impossible ambition. Our form of transport consisted of a motor cycle with a very boney pillion seat which I repeatedly decided never to mount again. It also had one of its usual punctures and the front tyre was as bald as an egg. My aunt's means of transport, a pre-war Morris Cowley which was only kept on the road by the ingenuity of her son, was in even worse condition in that it had developed a permanent leak in the roof and could only be driven in fine weather; the floorboards, particularly those beneath the feet of the back-seat passengers, had simply rotted away.

As I have said though, my aunt was a determined character, her son was resourceful and in this case she had useful allies: only the day before we had seen the name Newtownbarry on the map and decided it could not be far from that place called Tullow, so Peter and I decided it could do no harm for us to go along with them.

As is usual in Ireland, the fact that something out of the ordinary was about to take place generated an unusual brisk whirl of activity, a light-hearted certainty that although the auspices were surely hopeless, somehow or other they could be overcome.

It had rained during the night and my aunt's car leaked; due to the rotted floorboards, those sitting on the back seats would not be able to rest their feet on the floor, for fear of finding themselves skittering perilously along the roadway beneath. But my cousin had an answer for everything. In the toolshed he had discovered a large tin of something he told us was liquid rubber solution. Although the directions for use stated firmly that the surface on which it should be painted must be dry he proceeded to plaster it all over the roof. As for the floorboards he decided that the front doormat would at least protect the back-seat passengers from breaking their ankles or from being spattered from head to foot with mud. In no time at all every obstacle seemed to be overcome.

My aunt and I were installed in the back seat with our legs

firmly pressed against the two seats in front in order to spare the doormat. Peter was clutching a piece of string which did duty as a choke, my cousin swung the starting handle once, twice and the little engine sputtered to life. We were off, all was well and perhaps would have remained so, if, halfway to Athy, a mother duck accompanied by her five ducklings had not appeared suddenly out of a ditch and, in no hurry whatsoever, set off across the road.

My cousin suddenly applied the brakes, equally suddenly the world ahead of the windscreen disappeared behind an opaque film of white rubber solution, and my aunt and I found ourselves with our feet resting squarely on the road. Worse still, large white blobs raining down on us, drip by sticky drip, convinced us there was more than one leak in the roof.

I think, had it not been for the hand of fate and my aunt's Ancona hens, we would have decided to call off the whole expedition, for otherwise I do not know why it never occurred to us to do anything of the kind. Instead, to hell with the leaking roof; there was a bundle of old newspapers behind the back seat. My aunt and I considered ourselves rather adept at making paper hats when the children needed them for dressing-up; and anyway perhaps the deluge down the windscreen would not repeat itself now that warm sunshine, as happens so often in Ireland, had suddenly replaced the rain.

Four splendid three-cornered paper hats, four paper capes, and enough newspaper left to cover our knees, and if our motor car had been a Rolls-Royce and the paper hats festooned with plumes, my aunt, at least, could almost have passed for an admiral of the fleet setting off for some investiture at Buckingham Palace! As it was, of course, we could not have looked more ridiculous and, as we progressed at a sedate twenty-five miles per hour — the maximum speed attainable — through Athy and Castledermot and on towards Tullow, meeting perhaps two cars on the road, I could only wonder at the tactful acceptance displayed by those who greeted us in passing. The sideways shake of the head, the friendly smile, the touch of the cap, those customary Irish ways behind which I often sensed a quiet, calculating assessment of any situation. In our case, the motor car – however decrepit – must belong to gentry. Ah well, was it paper hats they were after wanting to parade around in this time? Long centuries had taught them how to cope with gentry, and paper hats were surely one of the less harmful of their many strange notions . . .

As we neared Tullow the landscape about us changed. No longer the rich grasslands of County Kildare, this was wilder country with unkempt fields of gorse and fern rising to heather-covered hills ahead of us – the Wicklow Mountains, deep blue in colour, the rain having ceased, and near now, very near. On asking for directions we were told to pass over two humps in the road, and Mr Dawson's would be the first farmer's place on the left. There was slight delay here: as we approached the house, a loud hissing sound, billowing clouds of steam and a barrage of assorted curses seemed to be coming from the cow-house. But when Peter and my cousin leapt out of the car, certain that we had arrived just in time to avert a crisis, they were met at the door by a cheerful old man wielding an empty bucket. It was the milking machine, so it was, as obstinate, impenitent a class of a yoke as had ever plagued a Christian. We must not disturb ourselves, it caught fire once a week, but he was well able for it, himself and a couple of buckets of water. If we were looking for the boss, he would allow he was in his office in Tullow Town.

Tullow, when we arrived there, was a quiet little town with a few small shops, a bank, and a turf accountant, watched over by the usual mossy statue of some long-dead patriot: this time he seemed to be a priest. There was not a motor car to be seen, just the odd pony trap or ass-cart, tied up in the square waiting patiently for their owners to emerge from one or other of the inevitable public houses which completed the scene.

Two church towers dominated the township, one Catholic and one Church of Ireland, both projecting a certain air of solid granite well-being, very obviously not shared by the members of their flock.

Paddy Dawson, the auctioneer, proved to be what is known in Ireland as 'a lovely man, God bless him'. To be such a person need have nothing to do with physical good looks, which he had, but honesty, kindness of heart and quickness of wit are essential to qualify. With Paddy there was a bonus, in that he possessed a certain quizzical spark in the eye, a sudden side glance just to show that the world was an odd sort of a place and you should never quite believe the tales that were in it. We later learned that, together with a Mr Flynn who owned a garage, he was the uncrowned king of the district.

Mr Dawson explained to us that the property he had for sale was in the townlands of Munny, or Money, an anglicized version of the original Irish *Muinebeag*, denoting a small wood. It had once been part of the four thousand acre Fitzwilliam estate, which had been expropriated by the British and stretched from Shilielagh to the sea. Munny lands consisted of four hundred and eighty acres and had been owned for the last hundred years by a family called Lawrenson. While the father was alive, it had been a showplace, for he had been an outstanding man. He had constructed a water course from the hills behind with such ingenuity that all his machinery for butter-making or turnip-chopping, could be driven by huge water wheels. The house and lands currently belonged to his son, who lived there with his two sisters and a younger brother. None of them had married, and they were now old and frail, and, as he explained, no longer able for it. It was no use pretending that it was a showplace any longer, for the lands had been let by conacre for years. Would it have a telephone perhaps? Ah now – electricity? – don't be talking. It was in fact a hardy sort of a place, but then Peter looked a hardy class of fellow.

We were so used to auctioneers waxing lyrical about the properties they had on their hands that Mr Dawson's description came as something of a relief, and since my aunt and my cousin had sputtered off towards Newtownbarry there seemed no harm in accepting his offer to drive us over and at least have a look at the place.

As we drove along the road to Shillelagh and turned off at a

143

cluster of cottages called the Coolkenna cross, the road became a rough track. A further mile or so and we reached what Mr Dawson laughingly described as the 'great gates': 'No longer in use,' he added rather unnecessarily, as it was hard to tell what could go on behind such a tangle of ivy and honeysuckle. A few yards further on, beside a high granite wall, there was a further entrance. No gates, great or small, this time, and after fifty yards or so the drive also petered out to become a muddy footpath. Ahead of us through bushes and undergrowth we could see a grey wall of battered stucco which we realized must be the house. Mr Dawson left us here explaining that he wanted to warn the old people of our unexpected arrival. He would go around to the back as the front door had gone the way of the great gates and was no longer in use.

It would be no use my pretending that we approached that back door with anything other than misgiving. The house was larger than we anticipated, larger and also nearer to disintegration. There seemed to be two kitchens, in one of which a large, dark, rather menacing-looking figure sat on a wooden stool before an open fire, over which were suspended some large rusty iron pots. She did not turn her head when we stood in the doorway, but remained staring into the flames, immobile except for her right arm, rhythmically turning an iron wheel which seemed to function as some kind of bellows. The second and larger kitchen was a shambles, dominated at the far end by the wreckage of a huge black kitchen range which looked as if it had been hit by a hand grenade.

Our arrival seemed to have caused some excitement, for as we stood talking with a small birdlike old lady whom Mr Dawson introduced to us as Miss Lottie, I could hear hurried footsteps above us, doors being slammed, and shutters flung open. Finally we were joined by the remaining members of the family, equally elderly, rather breathless, who were referred to as Master Ralphy, Miss Maggie and Master Dick.

An hour and a half later we drove back to Tullow in silence. I was silent because on my guided tour through that lonely, empty house with its peeling walls and tattered curtainings,

I thought to have seen a certain beauty hidden somewhere beneath the dust and decay. Peter, who meanwhile had walked over some of the lands, was also lost in thought, and I could believe that Mr Dawson's lack of any remark was due to his tact in allowing us time to get over the shock.

My aunt, my cousin, their motor car and the hens had not yet returned from Newtownbarry and it was not until Peter and I stood waiting for them in the town square, watched over by the benevolent eye of the local patriot, while the pony traps and the ass-carts dispersed to their various dwelling-places, that Peter put the question he had so often asked before: 'Well, what do you think of it?' The fact that I hesitated, probably showed him that he was going to be spared the usual shattering reply. 'I don't know,' I answered tentatively enough. 'What do you?' 'I don't know either really,' he said, 'there's such an awful lot of land and one walk around is simply not enough.' Then with *Teach Yourself Farming* in mind, he added, 'I would have to take soil samples of course and – and, well, soil samples . . .'

We paid two further visits to Munny House, in spite of the fact that Mr Dawson told us that the lands had been over exploited. They had been what is known as conacred for years, let for grazing on the eleven-month system: a deadly arrangement whereby local farmers removed all nourishment from the soil and nothing was ever given back to the land. We knew that this had come about because as Mr Dawson had explained the owners were simply 'not able for it', but as it proved they were still able to consume as much alcohol as the sale of their possessions could supply them with. When the furniture had gone and they were left with a table, four chairs, four beds, four trunks and a pony trap, they had cut down trees and sold them for firewood, and as soon as they learned that one Bangor slate could be exchanged for a bottle of Guinness they had immediately started on the roofs. When we arrived on the scene, however, they had luckily not progressed much further than part of the outhouses.

We knew, too, that because of Paddy Dawson's loyalty and

also that of their old herd, Will Byrne, the property was not in the hands of the Bank – 'The Bank', which since Ireland's freedom had taken over the power once wielded by British landlords.

'It was and it wasn't', had been Paddy Dawson's cryptic reply when we asked this all-important question. It was, on the one hand, because the Lawrensons owed £9,000 to the Bank; it wasn't, on the other hand, because whenever the Bank had tried to sell the property Will Byrne had stood resolutely at the entrance and warned any would-be buyers that no luck would go with it if they dared to open their mouths and make a bid. In Paddy Dawson's opinion the result was that the Bank was now also no longer able for it and might be only too willing to take a few hundred pounds in lieu of what they now recognized as being a hopelessly irretrievable debt.

In fact we had both fallen in love with the idea of buying Munny if, taking the soil tests and the state of the house and fencing into consideration, we could buy at a low enough price. But soil tested it had to be. Luckily Peter had met the son of a director of a big firm of maltsters who had studied agriculture. Peter asked him how one could set about taking and evaluating soil samples, a notion quite foreign to Ireland at the time. He told Peter that his father's firm employed such a man, Stephen Cullinan. With great enthusiasm, and delighted to be putting his science to practical use, Stephen worked very fast. After four days we had the result. The land was excessively acid, but it had a fair reserve of organic matter which could not rot to provide the necessary fertility because of the acidity. It needed vast quantities of lime and phosphate, but then it would produce anything. But the materials and the miles of new fencing needed would require a lot of money which we had to calculate as part of the purchase price.

Again we approached Paddy Dawson who, having had Munny on his books for some fifteen years, had no illusions about its value. He agreed to submit our offer of £4,500 to the owners who accepted without hesitation. We drew up the contract and made a down payment of a quarter of the price. We were to complete in February 1949.

On the day that we put down our deposit and after we left Paddy Dawson's office, awash with tea and warmed by messages of good luck, we decided to drive back towards Shillelagh and to have one more look at the home which would be ours if all the land deeds proved in order. We turned off at the Coolkenno crossroad and, as we approached the Munny lands, above the straggling hedgerows and the colourful boglands, I thought I saw one window of the old grey house peering down above the trees from the hill before us.

We turned in at the high grey wall and perforce stopped the motor cycle halfway up the track.

We did not wish to disturb the former owners but climbed over the fence and stood beneath a low wall which separated what must have once been a garden, from what we later knew to be the 'lawn field'.

As so often in Ireland, after a day of persistent rain, the sky was now cloudless as if washed clean, and the setting sun lit up the lands around us with an almost fluorescent radiance. Some of the great trees, the oaks and the elms, were already tinged with orange and with yellow, and stood out in meticulous detail against the purple background of the rolling Wicklow Mountains. In the far blue distance towered the highest peak of the Dublin Mountains, Lugnaquillia – 'mountain near the sun'.

Peter took my hand in his. 'Well, whatever the lands, whatever the poor old ruin,' he said, 'nothing, just nothing, can beat that view.'

Before leaving, I turned to look back towards the old grey house which we hoped would be our future home. Only that top dormer window could look back at me above the ragged yew trees and the tangled bushes, and I thought to myself, You've watched these trees being set in their places and you've watched them grow to such noble maturity, and you've watched the generations come and go; and now you've got a new lot to deal with, and I wonder what you think about it all.

147

Perhaps it was just a reflection of the setting sun, perhaps a simple reaction born of hope; but I thought to see a faint flicker of benevolence beam back at me over the bushes. Difficult to interpret really, except that, with luck, it might involve God's blessing; but then again being an Irish dormer window, it would equally include the equivocal after-thought that in this contrary world, whichever way it was, there would be divil a bit of harm in our chancing it.

Chapter Eleven

I HAD NO clear idea of what 'chancing it' might involve when some weeks later I arrived once more in Ireland to take up residence, so to speak.

Off and away once more, intent on opening a further chapter in our lives; this time one which would include trying to bridge a gulf which divides urban living from that of the yeoman farmer.

The day I chose to travel was 17th March, the feast day of St Patrick, celebrated with a tremendous show of blarneyfied enthusiasm, even to the downing of gallons of green beer by the descendants of those who had 'taken to the boats' in the last century and managed to reach the shores of America.

My childhood recollection of 'Paddy's Day', as celebrated in the homeland, was of a more muted affair altogether. Nothing more exciting than a few drab floats passing down O'Connell Street in Dublin, followed by a motley procession of – to me – very old men in caps and raincoats, who never seemed quite able to march in step. A saffron-kilted band thumping out patriotic airs with bagpipes and drums made a brief impression, but even this cheerful din fell silent as the cavalcade passed by the General Post Office, the GPO, symbol of the abortive uprising against the British in 1916. There a row of top-hatted figures stood to attention, perched on a rickety-looking platform which had obviously been erected for the occasion.

I was twelve years old at the time and, much against her principles, a good-natured aunt had been persuaded to take me to see the show. She was able to point out at least one of those figures as being President de Valera; tall, austere, and dressed in sombre black, he surveyed the passing procession through steel-rimmed spectacles with unsmiling severity. Only the tinkers, peddling the national emblem, seemed to be enjoying themselves in the side-streets, especially when, instead of the miniature shamrock, they managed to palm off a bunch of ordinary field clover on some unsuspecting customer.

I could not tell whether with the years, when celebrating their patron saint, the Republic of Ireland had managed to adopt at least one of their former rulers' virtues, which was a capacity to put on a really good show. But one thing that was certain was that on that day, as many 'exiles' as could fill the boats crossed the Irish Sea heading for 'the auld sod'. So my journey from London via the Mailboat from Holyhead to Dun Laoghaire looked like becoming long and uncomfortable and, as ever, bibulous and vocal.

In order to escape the rumpus I found my way to the usual sheltered corner on one of the upper decks where only wind and sea sounds and the rhythmic chugging of the ferry's engines disturbed the darkness and the quietness of the night.

I needed to be alone because just before leaving my family in England, when the furniture van stood before the door filled with what my mother assured me were easily dispensable 'bits and pieces', I had had a bad attack of cold feet. It could have been due to a sudden flashback memory of a parting which had taken place ten years before with everyone trying to be so cheerful. 'Good luck, Chris', 'See you soon, darling', until the final 'Goodbye – goodbye', with the kisses and the hugs and the waving hands. Then I was leaving for Germany, war was pending, and it was to be six long years and too many

150

other farewells before I saw them all again. Now, although self-analysis was not one of my usual habits, there must have been something about the regular chugging of those Mailboat engines which triggered off my apprehension. How would it be?

We would no longer be townsfolk whose means of transport could be a bus, a train, or a motor car, and whose daily needs could be supplied by the shop around the corner, who could head for the country at weekends to sniff the air and pause awhile to contemplate the peaceful scene of cows grazing lush green pastures or to watch little lambs frolicking in the fields under the watchful eye of their placid mothers. Instead, we would be joining up with those whose livelihoods depended on whether those lambs lived and thrived, or wilted and died, and on milking those cows rain or shine from Monday morning through to Sunday eve in order that others, referred to with scant respect as 'townees', should find their morning milk in bottles on their doorsteps.

I could reckon that although our attitude towards life as farmers of the land was probably tinged with romanticism, we were all in good health and well equipped for our new venture. Except for my spell in the Black Forest, all that I knew of the country life was extreme comfort, with gardeners busy at the lawns and flowerbeds, and a household so well equipped with domestics that my mother, more honest than her pampered offspring, once declared that she wondered what we did all day.

Why the sudden panic? Simply perhaps that I was older now, beginning to recognize just how little I really knew about Ireland and that to remember it simply as a happy-go-lucky playground would not be enough. The regular chugging of the Mailboat's engines reminded me of a certain trait in my own make-up, my innate inability to maintain a rhythm of non-stop undiluted purposefulness. Instead I found it all too easy to wander from a central theme, to stray from the path, searching the horizon for something new, curious to discover what could lie over the brow of any hill. '*A penny for your thoughts – pay attention, Christabel!*' It was surely a liability, but well compensated by a sturdy optimism, always ready to assure me that whatever awaited my wide-eyed arrival would probably be something rather nice.

The darkness was fading into a dawn glow and the ship's engines were gradually slowing down. Some time back I thought to have picked out a shadowy contour and sensed the nearness of land. One of the outer islands perhaps; could be Ireland's Eye.

But the morning was bitterly cold and for some time I had been regretting my decision to send my anorak off in the furniture van. Instead, for no reason I can think of, I had decided to doll myself up as if heading for some civic reception in black and pale blue, with a hat which, with some imagination, I felt made me look like Greta Garbo in her film, *Anna Karenina*. The result: I was simply freezing! So I made for the lower decks which I found to be already alive with the excitement of imminent arrival. Bundles and bags, babies in arms and rolls of bedding. When the Irish come home they do it in quantity and style, and to judge from the waving, welcoming crowds, half the island turns out on the quayside to greet them.

I could see my special bit of Ireland, standing almost head and shoulders above the rest, waiting quietly near the gang plank. It was almost a relief when after the warmest of welcomes one of the first things Peter asked me was whether I had remembered to bring with me a bag of something called cobalt, unobtainable in Ireland, but seemingly essential to our future livelihood. A relief, because even if I had not been able to answer with supreme confidence that the stuff was coming along in the furniture van, I could be reassured that the much-needed, non-stop, undiluted purposefulness part of the bargain was in good shape.

Over a splendid breakfast in a Victorian edifice which overlooked the harbour, a hotel which had undoubtedly given comfort to many a seasick traveller, and from the state of the décor possibly even to Queen Victoria herself, Greta Garbo hats were soon forgotten. I could see that, for the first time since his accident, Peter had become completely involved in what was still to me a new and unknown world.

While I was trying to fix up affairs in England, Peter was living in Munny together with its former owners, as the inimitable Paddy Dawson tried to find them a house suitable to their means. He had managed to do so a fortnight before my arrival, and, to celebrate their departure, a giant auction had taken place on the premises. Fair days and auctions, it would seem, along with church going and Mass on Sundays, were social occasions not to be missed by the scattered country folk who lived about us. There could not have been much to collect but just the same a cavalcade of bicycles, pony traps, ass-carts and even the odd ancient tractor turned up to join the fun and also doubtless take a look at 'them Germans', who were now the owners of 'the Big House'. Nothing much to collect, but urged on by Paddy Dawson, nuts and bolts, leaking buckets, ladders with missing rungs, tattered curtains and even some pots of paint and brushes which Peter had bought in the hope of doing some decorating before my arrival, were carted away, along with the *pièce de résistance*, in the form of a donkey. The donkey, it seemed, was a particular attraction in the district, as its task in life had been to take Kate, our predecessors' factotum, to Mass on Sundays. She seldom arrived on time, because whenever she was greeted on her journey by friendly neighbours well used to the game, it stopped stone dead. 'Grand day, Kate,' was enough, and it took at least ten minutes to get Kate, the ass-cart, and the donkey, into motion once again.

Peter could tell me that, to add to our assets, we now also had allies. There was Michael Noctor, whose parents had been with some of my relations as housekeeper and gardener, and had carried on stoically as the big house began to crumble and the garden threatened to become a wilderness. Michael, their second son, had decided to risk leaving the rich farmlands of Kildare and to join us in County Wicklow, which was to him a foreign country. With him had come the daughter of a neighbour, who warned us, accurately it was to prove, that her knowledge of cooking was 'anarchic'. But Molly, as was her name, had taken charge of the iron pots and pans suspended over the open fire and could produce what she called a 'cake of bread' from under the ashes, which Peter declared was the nearest thing to *Vollkornbrot* he had tasted since leaving Germany.

There was also the gallant Will Byrne who had spent his working life as herd to the former owners of Munny, and as they sank deeper into debt had kept prospective buyers at bay. Lastly, there was Stephen Cullinan. Stephen, who had taken the soil samples, came from one of those indomitable Irish families evicted to the West of Ireland, 'to hell or to Connaught', by English landowners. He was one of six sons and two daughters, all reared on the patch of rock and bogland which had been allotted to them. All had survived and made good. His brothers, those who had not 'taken to the boats' as the journey to America was known at the time, had become engineers and civil servants, his sisters nuns or nurses. Stephen himself had become an agricultural chemist, and when we met him he was living in cramped quarters in Athy, County Kildare, employed for a pittance by the firm of maltsters. In spite of his splendid looks, with his shock of curly dark hair and the green-blue eyes so often to be found in the West, Stephen's health was delicate, with bouts of asthma which were surely not alleviated by his mode of living. Nothing, however, could dim his enthusiasm. 'Look after the land and the land will look after you', was his dictum, learned at his father's knee, and as soon as he heard we were buying the derelict farm in the Wicklow Mountains, he volunteered to join us and advise us on how to proceed.

While filling me in on all the details, Peter was talking so much and at such speed that I was finding it quite hard to swallow my excellent breakfast. When he arrived at the result of Stephen's investigations, pH this and pH that, the chemical terms he used sounded most professional. But, as far as I could gather, they indicated that because of constant neglect, constant over-grazing and over-cropping, no fertility whatsoever was left in the soil we were supposed to till, reap and harvest. So I thought I had better eat up quickly as it looked as if it might be the last square meal I would have for months.

Leaving Dublin behind us, the van, devoid of a single spring, leapt boisterously from one pothole to the next, and Peter explained to me, between gasps, that when he left Munny at 5 o'clock that morning, he had not been too happy about the situation he had left behind.

All of our allies, including of course *Teach Yourself Farming*, had made it clear that in order to make a start on very little capital, we would have to invest in a herd of milking cows. Larger sums of money from beef and sheep and hoped-for corn crops would only reach the bank account at irregular intervals, whereas a milk cheque would arrive by the month and thus help pay the wages and keep us financially afloat.

It was this future milking herd that was causing Peter concern. He had bought about eight heifers, all in calf, and they had been delivered by lorry the previous day. During the night, he had heard curious noises coming from the cow-house, and before he left Michael confirmed that at least two of the expectant ladies had not enjoyed the cross-country journey by lorry, and were well on the way to producing their offspring. At 5 o'clock that morning Peter had had to leave Michael coping alone with the situation, and as we bounced up the drive and came to a dead stop outside the cow-house, even I could understand from the grunts and groans, the rattling of chains and the stamping of hooves, that the situation inside might be out of hand. Peter leapt out of the van, dragged off his jacket, and, in spite of my finery, I thought best to follow suit.

Having been brought up in the aforementioned 'stiff upper lip' tradition, I shall describe the sight which met my eyes as I gingerly put my head round the cow-house only as a somewhat crude introduction to country life.

The straw strewn about the floor was a mass of blood mixed up with some shining mess which I afterwards learned was the afterbirth. Two of the row of animals before me obviously had their ordeal behind them and were busily licking their calves, one of which had already struggled to its feet and discovered the milk supply. The rest had decided to follow their good example, but had not as yet been so successful. They were, in fact, still hard at it, so that forefeet, heads, half-heads, and, in one case, something which looked rather like a tail, were vigorously trying to churn their way into the world. Poor Michael, also well spattered with blood and armed with a rope, was obviously exhausted, but as Peter pulled off his jacket and plunged into the fray, he managed to smile, bid me welcome, and remark that the way it was, it looked as if we were in for some class of a struggle.

According to Michael, it seemed that it was necessary to sprinkle salt on the heads of newly born calves in order to encourage their mothers to lick them dry, so, when Peter yelled for more salt, I was only too glad to retire hurriedly and see if I could find it up in the house. In truth, if the thought of myself standing there all dressed up and probably pea-green in the face had not suddenly struck me as extremely funny, the *mise-en-scène* before me, combined with the pungent smell of creation, was well on the way to making me feel extremely sick.

A narrow pathway, cleared of grass and undergrowth, led me to the house and to the front door, which only needed a sharp kick to push it open, and I found I was standing in the hallway which no longer seemed so dark as when I had been there before. Dark red with the occasional purple blotch had been the colour scheme favoured by our predecessors, but Peter must have used whatever paint he had managed to rescue from the farm auction, for the walls were now white. He had not managed the staircase, but no amount of dark brown veneer could hide its graceful curves as it wound its way up to the floor above. Only a row of assorted buckets, some half-filled with water, and lined up from one step to the next, made me pause a moment to conclude that they could only be explained away by the absence of so many slates from the roof.

As I stood there in the echoing carpetless hallway, looking about me, my eyes wandering over the well-laid floorboards, the fine mahogany doorways so liberally spattered with worm holes, a curious thought occurred to me. Could it have been some racial memory, some chance anecdote, some sudden reminiscence conjured up by my father when rustling through family papers, which had induced me to try and dress the part of châtelaine? How had they behaved, those Anglo-Irish ancestors of mine, during the various rebellions, the famines, the occupation of an island geographically so close at hand, racially so remote? Had there been pity when the native Irish died of hunger in their thousands or left by the boatload for America? As I had never before actually lived here, I felt myself to be free of the 'Big House' syndrome. Bother the worm holes and the buckets on the stairs; for me, for us, I decided it was all going to be different.

It was Molly's gentle voice bidding me welcome, invoking God's blessing on us and the house which brought me back to the present realities, for she added that the kettle was boiling on the hob and she was 'allowing' the boss man, and Michael would be needing a cup of tea when the performance outside was behind them.

Salt — of course, it was salt they needed, and, if my extra smart get-up had anything to do with ancestral memories, I felt this was the moment to cast them aside. To hell with worm holes!

A pair of wellington boots and a raincoat seemed to be doing nothing useful in the hall, so I kicked off my shoes, discarded my black and pale blue ensemble, dropped my Greta Garbo hat into one of the empty buckets, and with my glowing desire to blaze a trail dimmed only temporarily, I followed Molly into the kitchen where she supplied me with a drum of salt and let me out of the back door into the yard.

Chapter Twelve

'A SATISFACTORY TERM'S *work – Christabel is settling in nicely.*' Anyone acquainted with the British educational system would recognize the well-worn phrasing as all over England children sentenced to boarding-school, when most of them would have been far happier at home, were doubtless trying to do just that. I had so often read the wording on my own, my sister's, brothers' and sons' school reports, and sometimes wondered if it had not been conceived by weary pedagogues simply to pacify anxious, possibly guilt-ridden parents.

The settling-in process at Munny was very different, involving nothing so passive as settling-down, but rather scenes which stand out in my memory like flash-light photographs, some surprising, some inspiring, some disconcerting, some hilarious; all milestones along our chosen road, as we advanced from cows to beef cattle and to sheep; from sparse crops of oats, cut with a binder, stooked and threshed, to respectable harvests of barley and wheat, blown into trailers by a combine harvester.

The school holidays in the spring of 1949 were, for me, a joyous prelude to all this activity. There must be an element of the broody hen in my make-up, for I was well aware that my main reason for happiness came from having all my family under one roof, something which had not been the case since bombs drove us out of Berlin. I could not excel myself in the garden, for when I wrote to my expert mother for advice, her reply was to wait awhile before planting to see what came up. The summer passed and nothing whatsoever did come up, except a forest of Jerusalem artichokes which could have provided us with enough soup to last a lifetime.

Nevertheless I remained deeply content, for the leaking roof I knew to be our very own, the bath-tub, our bath-tub, and the tangled scrub outside maybe our future garden. I could even imagine that the old grey mansion itself, with its glorious view over the hills, could be joining in the fun. It might be listening with pleasure to our irrepressible sons sliding down the banisters and clattering up and down its long carpetless passageways, or sharing our astonishment when we tried to run a bath and water flowed from those splendid taps but was accompanied by an assortment of incomplete frogs and a steady flow of tadpoles.

If I allowed my imagination to run wild, I could even picture those crumbling walls urging us on to greater effort, hoping perhaps to return one day to a long-lost eighteenth-century elegance.

While the boys were busy at what they called exploring everything and I at what Peter described as nest-building, he was applying himself with untiring energy to what was to become his 'Four-Year Plan'. Stephen Cullinan, Paddy Dawson and *Teach Yourself Farming* were his constant advisors.

Cows, well why not? The gay yodelling of cowherds and the delicate tinkle of cowbells returning from the high pastures in the Black Forest still echoed in my ears. And what about the 'Daisies', the 'Buttercups' and the 'Rosebuds', docile friends all eager to provide fresh milk and butter for the household?

Wait till I tell you! Anyone who might entertain romantic ideas as to the role of the cow in farming family life and who expects harmony to prevail would be wise to drop them forthwith. For there is something utterly dispiriting about milking a lot of cows morning and evening, Monday to Sunday, January to December.

In the nature of things, a cow's lactation does not go on for ever, so that, even if not overtaken by milk fever or mastitis, her supply of milk slowly dries up, the graph on the wall curves downwards, and the humour of the attendant cowman follows suit. When he then lugs increasingly fewer cans down the road, and heaves them onto the milk stand to await collection, he can only think with deepening gloom of that dwindling milk cheque. It cannot be long before such sympathetic noises as, 'Oh dear – bad luck, never mind' soon dry up likewise.

As for a bull, although appreciating the necessity, I had visions of bull fighters being tossed about like discarded dolls; although not wishing to disturb the 'Four-Year Plan' I decided that no bull was going to rampage about our hedgeless, gateless, unprotected fields. I only relented when assured that this ferocious addition to our menagerie would be confined to just one paddock, so fenced in, so enclosed as to resemble an impregnable fortress. One of those impregnable fortresses you can read about no doubt, for it was only a matter of days before, called outside to consult with our local Garda about a gun licence, I and the bull met up with each other face to face. Obviously no heroine, I only had time to screech, 'The bull's out' before scooting back into the house. Although I could not reach the roof, I still managed to arrive in record time at a top-floor window from whence I could witness our arm of the law, gun licence forgotten, pedalling his ancient bicycle away down the drive at break-neck speed, while my courageous, but surely doomed, husband, armed with a golf umbrella, somehow succeeded in bluffing the animal to retreat backwards into an outhouse.

My hunch about cows became conviction after Peter von Mentzingen joined our team for a full year and became as another son to us. Peter was strong and extremely handsome with a delightful sense of humour and as he was due to inherit an estate in Württemberg which, having a castle attached might include plenty of debts, he was well aware of the importance of the monthly milk cheque. It took some time for the cow-house to have its effect on this cheerful boy. For many weeks he entered into the spirit of the game, welcoming them in from the field, watching with amusement as they pushed their way into their favourite stalls, whistling to himself as he washed down their udders before applying the milking machine and driving them out again with an affectionate slap on the haunches. Yet one morning, as I passed through the yard, I found him leaning against the cow-house door staring disconsolately into the distance, with the usual river of liquid manure flowing round his boots. 'Bally old Brünhilde's let me down today, Chris,' he said and added 'I'm afraid it'll have to be cows when I get back again to Germany. German cows, but I guess they are the same all over the world.'

I had to admit that I had no idea how German cows behaved, but could well believe that, rather than goose-stepping into the cow-house they would jostle and kick, get mastitis and lash out with their tails at exactly the wrong moment, just like every other cow. As we strolled back together to the house, although, as ever, not wishing to disturb my husband's 'Four-Year Plan', I knew I was on my way to coming to a firm decision. It might need a bit of time but a few hints, some more forceful than others, should do the trick as far as I was concerned: the cows, the chugging of the milking machine, all the paraphernalia required to put a bottle of milk on a stranger's doorstep would, as soon as we could afford it, be past history.

Peter von Mentzingen went back to Germany, inherited his castle and married a lovely girl. When we visited him we were able to report that our cows now reared their own calves, single suckling being the order of the day. We could also take note that Peter had taken to breeding horses. Bidding goodbye to our milking herd had been far easier than expected as by then we had all reached the stage of hardly being able to wait for our milk contract to expire. The first phase of the 'Four-Year Plan' had come to a successful end.

Something however had to make up for what even I was beginning to refer to as our cash flow. It was decided that it must be more grain growing and the addition of sheep which meant attending a sheep and cattle fair. Fair days in Tullow took place once a month, on a Monday, when the little town was invaded by local farmers and their families, accompanied by their means of livelihood. Prudent shopkeepers boarded up their doors and windows while cows, bullocks, heifers and calves, ponies and donkeys took over the main street, flooding it in no time with slithery rivers of greenish muck. No one allowed this to disturb the main business of the day, nor the general air of cheerful sociability, which I once heard described with enthusiasm as being 'as good as a wake'. In those days banks played little role in business deals as no one wished for 'them fellows in their shirts and ties' to be poking around in affairs that were private. Instead, a spit on the palm and a handshake were enough to seal a bargain, after which those shopkeepers who happened to have a 'Select Lounge' tucked away in their back premises came into their own. They could remove the barricade and be assured of profiting in their own fashion from the subsequent celebrations. In the evening of those market days a little cattle train chugged down the track towards Dublin and our town returned to normality once again.

My own experience of such a day in Tullow was unusual in that, still innocent of what might be outside the bounds of possibility, I chose to go to the hairdresser and was sitting under the drier reading peacefully when a disturbance made me glance in the mirror and I realized I was not alone in my cubicle: I had been joined by a bullock, or it could have been a heifer. The animal gazed at me placidly for a moment or two before retreating backwards through the curtains, seeming to understand that it had come to the wrong address. 'Mary, Mother of God – would you know,' laughed the hairdresser as she saw it off the premises, and I gathered that this was not the first time she had dealt with such an unusual client.

Peter's visit to the market was of more consequence,

although the result was no less disconcerting when he returned home the proud and innocent owner of a certain breed of sheep known as 'Hornies'. Rural communication can surely only be equalled by the African drum-beat for everyone he met in the market square that day seemed to know he was 'after sheep'. Before long, he was approached by a persuasive old hand at the game, who soon convinced him that if he was looking for a real bargain, hardy, prolific, and above all, not too expensive, he could offer him the real thing. The fact that in order to inspect this attractive proposition he would have to accompany the owner to a distant hilltop, should, I suppose, have sounded an alarm signal. The farming world being what it is, it would have been unnatural for the owner to explain that his sheep were only suitable for mountain grazing and that hedges, fences and ditches, even five-bar gates, were child's play should one purposeful animal decide to break out. It would then be followed, almost immediately, by its baaing, bleating, companions, all heading for some unknown reason towards some other grazing ground.

'They're on the move,' became Peter's rallying cry, as the usual hullabaloo reached our ears and had us whooping and charging about the place, as often as not in our night-clothes, in an abortive effort to keep those hornies off our crops.

I suppose anyone brought up on the land could have told us that when dealing with sheep, whooping and charging around the place was a recipe for disaster, and that when lacking a sheep-dog, man should make a quiet, almost uninterested, approach. Patience, much patience, would then be needed before a leader made up its mind to venture off in the desired direction, when with luck the remainder of the flock would obediently follow suit. Quite simple really, but just one of those lessons to be learned the hard way by a former student of the Law and one clueless woman who had once prided herself on having won a scholarship to Oxford University.

I have to admit that by the time those hornies departed and were replaced by a less adventurous breed, my interest in sheep, apart from the financial virtues, had reached another low ebb.

It was not their fault that, in my opinion, they possessed the dumbest, glummest faces on earth, but it was beyond me why they could not stay put. Why lie down and die at the drop of a hat, or, in snow, head with deadly purpose for the nearest snow-drift and allow themselves to be buried alive?

I suppose it is about time I admitted to not being a natural devotee of farm animals, and therefore needed occasional encouragement. It came my way on a glorious April day when the lambing season was in full swing.

She was lying near the gate, with Michael beside her, that yellow-eyed ewe who was struggling with a breech birth and whose efforts were getting weaker by the minute. It must have been the look she gave me. 'Don't just stand there,' she seemed to be pleading as her eyes glazed over in agony. 'You're a woman too, can't you see what I am going through? Give us a hand, for God's sake.'

I glanced at Michael standing helplessly by with his bucket of Jeyes Fluid and his lump of Pears soap and his dilemma came to me in a flash. He had tried to turn the lamb and bring it into the world right way round but his hand was too big. I glanced at my own and without quite knowing how I was to go about it, I found myself muttering, 'Come on, old girl, I'm with you,' as I rolled up my sleeve, delved my arm into the bucket, soaked it well and proceeded to go about my business. 'I'm with you,' but in truth once inside I had little idea where I was; from then on, the assortment of slithery heads and legs, fore and aft, was completely bewildering. I was lucky that day, as the ewe had been through it before and the head and forelegs I managed to get a grip on happened to belong to each other. A steady pull and the miracle happened. A lamb had been born and I was midwife. 'It could be twins, it could be triplets, mam, so it could!' Michael was smiling, too, as he wiped its face, held it upside down and smacked it smartly until it sneezed. Twins? – Triplets? I was ready for anything, and by the time I had delivered number three, that first born was struggling to its feet nosing around for the milk supply.

Just a fleeting moment in time when the skies clear and

mists are swept away. 'Carved in God's image or something, that's what we both are, see?' I could assure my woolly companion rather breathlessly as we lay there resting up against each other in a pool of mud and blood.

I would like to be able to say that besides becoming rather an expert as a midwife, I played a significant role where further farming activities were concerned. Would I ever become a worthwhile farmer's wife? I had to doubt it, for to judge by some of our more professional neighbours, a farmer's wife needed to be a prodigy in order to consider herself worthy of her salt. Besides keeping her family fed and clothed, rearing the calves, possibly some piglets, tending the vegetable patch and hustling to the rescue when crises occurred, if she ever had time to sit down and read, she must learn how to bake special cakes, make special jams, so that the sight of an unripe tomato would be enough to ensure her directing what remained of her energy towards tasty pickles, preserves and chutneys.

But I was determined to make my contribution and decided to plump for hens, mainly, I think, because Christopher was still at an age when finding eggs in a nest is an exciting and satisfying experience. He was six when we came to Munny, and had left his days in boarding-school, temporarily at least, behind him. Much of his time was now spent trudging back and forth to the local school where a charming young teacher tried to instil some learning into a group of Protestant children between the ages of six and fourteen. As far as our son was concerned, she had not got much beyond persuading him to recite the Lord's Prayer, at the top of his voice, with a splendid Irish accent, and to knit me a golliwog for Christmas; but feeding those hens and collecting the eggs was a job he took very seriously.

It was, therefore, a major tragedy when a friend who had taken an early morning stroll returned to breakfast with downcast eye and advised me not to go near the hen paddock. A fox had obviously invaded my hen-run in the night, and except for a few mutilated corpses, there was no longer a hen to be seen.

I must have had some affection for those birds as it took me two days, and the removal of the bodies, before I could take Christopher by the hand and with him face up to their deserted home. As I looked about me, wondering why it should be that not only certain humans, but also animals seem to kill for fun, I heard a faint sound, the rustling of leaves, coming from an upper branch of one of the surrounding trees. There, sure enough, with head sunk in its feathers and somewhat rocky on its legs, was perched one of my hens, obviously a sole survivor. We were delighted to see her and Christopher was about to run off and fetch her some food when she fluttered to the ground, landed like a stone and suddenly let out a resounding whoop, a joyful crow, unmistakably that of a cock. 'Gosh! Mum, what's that?' Christopher stopped in his tracks, turned to me and seeing the expression on my face, burst out laughing. What's that? A good question, and certainly one for which I had no answer. *Teach Yourself Poultry* had certainly not mentioned that the fright of a lifetime could spark off a sex change for a hen.

We set about trying to woo our sole survivor back to becoming a hen again by sitting it on some eggs. It responded for a while, only to ruin its chance of ever rearing a family by forgetting about them every morning in order to greet the dawn with its newly discovered trumpet call. Thinking perhaps that it was lonely we introduced it to three ducks, but it was not long before they became fed-up with its behaviour and fled in panic as soon as he/she approached them with a purposeful glint in its eye.

The veterinary profession provided no answer, and doubting if Herr Freud had ever applied himself to the problem of the bisexual hen, we finally left her to her bizarre lifestyle until she died a natural death. Only Christopher was satisfied at being able to inform a spellbound school audience that one of his charges up on the farm could surely qualify for a world record.

When my thoughts turn to those early years in Munny, one vivid memory chases another. I sit in comfort and warmth; I switch on the light and switch it off again; I go to the telephone and chat with a friend or a neighbour should I so wish. If I look back over my shoulder though, just behind me, is a small oil lamp casting weird shadows on the wall and beside it a fizzing flaring 'Tilley', last witness to the only blazing row about our finances that Peter and I ever had, when I bought the wretched thing without first consulting his 'Four-Year Plan'!

Our initial introduction to what was known in those days as 'the Electric' came from someone who was known in the district as 'a great man with the wires'. He installed a generator, six old bus batteries and two extra light bulbs for the house. We were only plunged back into darkness when all available light was needed for the milking machine and as this could happen quite suddenly it was wise to keep a candle close at hand. The expert with the wires made only one mistake when trying to extend his territory to include the pig-house, which contained two sows destined, along with their offspring, to make a fortune for our eldest son, Nicky.

On their way back to pasture, the cows had to pass the pig-house door and they had not done so more than twice when our cowman of the day declared he would no longer stay with us as the place was haunted. 'Lepping around, sir, and that scared as if the Divil had them by the tail,' he exclaimed and was about to launch into one of the many horror tales which are rife in all lonely country places, when Peter persuaded him to drive all the cows back again into the yard. Sure enough, as they passed the pig-house they launched themselves into what looked like a parody of some ritual dance, legs up, knees up, head down, tails up, a bovine jam session, which would have been awe-inspiring if some of the participants had not been in an obvious state of near panic. Needless to relate, wet hooves, and too lightly insulated wiring laid just an inch below the ground, soon solved the mystery of our haunted farmyard.

The day came at last when rumour had it that the mains supply was described as advancing on us all the way from Dublin or it could be Cork, or might be Limerick; no matter, such was the enthusiasm that it was not easy to dissuade the Electricity Board from placing a huge pylon right beside our front door.

However, with tact, another crisis was avoided and we could switch those lights on and off, off and on, upstairs and downstairs, all over the place, transforming at will our not so stately home into a fairyland.

I was to discover that one of the many attractions of living in Ireland for anyone with a disorderly mind is the lack of need to waste time wondering if, how, why or when certain happenings, certain predictable events, will take place; they might so they might, but they also might not, you could never be quite sure.

For instance, I often wondered how many artless tourists, ignorant of the national game of playing about with signposts, and therefore much confused, have spent further hours trying to reach their destination by simply stopping and asking the way. Charmed then by the friendly solicitude of their informant, told to wheel this way, to wheel that, how could they know as they continued their journey smiling so gratefully, that a widespread difficulty in distinguishing the right hand from the left had more than likely sent them off once more in the wrong direction?

'A chara – mise le meas', after spending many useless hours in the grocer's store waiting for temperamental telephone calls, I used up my five words of Irish hoping to show enough respect to apply to the Department of Posts and Telegraphs for a private line. No one seemed much impressed with my patriotic effort but after several months I did receive a reply, letting me know that the installation of such a luxury would cost us an initial outlay of £350.00. We were not feeling too affluent at the time so decided with regret to postpone things for another day. Imagine my surprise, when, en route for the Post Office some days later, I passed a lively crew of postal engineers well equipped with ladders, wires and poles, digging holes and lopping off branches, obviously bent on bringing a telephone up to our door. Nor was that the end of it, for it was not to be too long before we were supplied with two telephones. The first was a period piece, with a crank handle, which when turned at speed alerted the postmistress into setting off on her voyage along the wires to whatever number we required. This was soon joined by another with a numbered dial. Ireland had joined the EEC, the 'dialling' was upon us, and we were assured that once the new arrival was fixed up and had settled down, we would find ourselves talking to 'the whole wide world'.

Sure enough, one year later, almost to the day, this information proved to be correct. Well, perhaps not quite correct, but by following the instructions sent to us in the post, by turning the dial slowly and methodically and by ignoring certain noises which made us wonder if the grandfather clock was advancing upon us from the kitchen, whichever way we dialled we could find ourselves talking to a host of people we had never met or heard of in our lives before.

Some seemed unduly upset at our intrusion into what might have been a business call of some urgency; others quite willing to pass a few minutes of the day in friendly chat with a stranger. Only one poor lady from Donegal hung up on us after declaring that the whole country was in a heap anyway and she was off to America. On a further occasion, having dialled as I thought a Dublin number, I was answered by the cheerful voice of our linesman 'working on the line,' he said, and we could even exchange witticisms, agreeing with each other whole-heartedly that he was not the only one who was 'up the pole'.

Why was it then that in spite of all this progress we felt a sense of loss when our old friend with the crank handle was declared redundant and we were given to understand that the friendly voice of the postmistress must also go off the air; nor when the line crackled, threatened to burst our eardrums and go dead as heretofore, could we sally forth with a long pole and bash away at the wires until we were on the air again.

We were not alone in our temporary fit of the dumps for I had to think of those many local ladies who kept the wheels of Irish rural industry turning; who sat unperturbed beside minute electric fires in back-room offices buffeted by gale-force draughts, and of the one who confessed it would be 'awful lonesome' once the dialling took over. No more heart-to-hearts for free with friends on the local switchboards, no more crossed lines to give one the opportunity of keeping abreast with local and even national affairs. For some progress just looked like being awful lonesome.

For me progress was a light bulb and some books, all luxuries I had been unable to indulge in simultaneously for years.

I would probably have been better occupied if I had followed Peter's good example, tried to stick to my present role as farmer's wife, and looked for a booklet entitled *Teach Yourself How To Love Cows, Sheep, Cats and Dogs*, but instead, I steered my lone course towards contemporary Irish history. Needless to say I was unaware of how many before me had tried to make sense of the subject and failed, nor was it to be long before I joined their bewildered ranks.

Chapter Thirteen

IRELAND UNITED GAELIC and Free. When surveying the events in Ireland of the 1950s and the 1960s the history books could proudly proclaim these decades as having witnessed the Republic's great leap forward from a small, partly dependent state, intimately, almost incestuously, involved with its own affairs, to a new outward-looking Ireland freed from the last threads of British rule, outside the Commonwealth, eager to plan its own destiny and to play a role in international affairs.

Ulster, Munster, Leinster and Connaught, the 'Four Green Fields', the only cloud on such a glowing horizon being the awkward fact that one of those green fields still stubbornly refused to be drawn in, preferring with iron determination to remain outside the fence.

Why? Protestants to the North, Catholics to the South of a carelessly drawn borderline dividing neighbour from neighbour, farmhouse from farmlands, but, above all, dyed-in-the-wool Protestants from equally rigid Catholics. It was thus the so-called 'Troubles' had been born and as yet seemed to have found no solution.

There was no use denying that the Catholic Church, 'the

Faith', had kept an educational ethic alive in Ireland in times of great hardship, providing the famous 'hedge schools' when the Irish were banned from schooling by their British overlords. In those times of worldly suffering, too, it had provided the escape route to a blissful hereafter. But now it held the stage and the bigotry displayed on each side of a straggling North-South border was beyond my comprehension.

This was the situation which had existed for so many decades in Ireland; one which I could not help fearing might ultimately tear the little country apart. It was one which I hoped at least to clarify, ensconced in our only armchair with the written word and plenty of cigarettes to hand, and that almost audible silence about me which belongs to long winter evenings in the country. I soon discovered that I was not too well equipped for my self-appointed task, for my own liberal upbringing in England had not included differentiating between Catholic and Protestant, Jew and Gentile, and my experience of Hitler's regime in Germany had given me a loathing of racial or religious discrimination of any kind. During those Nazi years the scenario had been so different. It was a time when the churches — Protestant and Catholic — were united against a common enemy.

There was Claus von Stauffenberg, a devout Catholic, who had asked for and been granted dispensation by his priest before setting off for Hitler's Army Headquarters in order to rid the world of a monster he believed to be an Anti-Christ. Both were to die, as was one of my heroes, Father Delp, who turned to his persecutors before being hanged and remarked with serenity 'In a few minutes' time I will know for certain what many of you may be wondering about.'

There was Graf Galen, the Catholic Archbishop of Cologne (Münster), whose sermons and pastoral letters were passed avidly from ear to ear, from hand to hand, no matter whether Catholic or Protestant; and the Lutheran Pastors, Niemöller and Bonhœffer, whose messages from prison did likewise. To me all this had nothing to do with churches, statues or monuments, but signified the true strength of Christianity as I believed it should be.

I therefore found myself becoming increasingly dismayed to find that in this so-called 'free democracy', the ethics and moral teachings of one church – the Roman Catholic Church – represented by the hierarchy of bishops, could not only hold such powerful sway over the lives of their own Catholic flock, but that their authority extended to include everyone who happened to live in what had become the 'Republic of Ireland'.

Since 1937, a Censorship of Publications Act, which included theatrical plays and films, had reached the Statute Book, and Censorship Boards, mostly chaired by a member of the priesthood, were firmly entrenched, having succeeded in banning the works of many outstanding authors of the day. The quality of some judgements made could be measured when a learned tome on soil erosion, with the unfortunate title *Rape Around Our Shores*, never reached the bookshelves. When it came to films, a visit to the local cinema often included a challenge to the imagination, for as soon as the screen portrayed sex, even in its most innocent form, out came the censor's scissors. A snip, a blank, and a bewildered audience could find themselves transported post-haste to safer and less controversial territory. The Public Dance Hall Act of 1929 saw to it that such entertainment could only take place under the watchful eye of a priest, whose role was to convince himself, and his superiors, that, in between dances, the width of the dance floor divided the would-be revellers, the boys from the girls.

Divorce and birth control by any means other than abstinence were dealt with under a so-called Criminal Law Amendment Act, later to be enshrined in the Constitution. In the case of divorce, something had come unstuck; the State, by forbidding it under any circumstances, found itself limping along well behind the Church, which in certain cases could grant an annulment of marriage. It could do so by conveniently overlooking the paradoxical position of any children born to such a union, declaring quite simply that the marriage had

173

never been consummated. For a Catholic to attend Trinity College, Dublin, the oldest university in the land, founded some four hundred years ago by Queen Elizabeth I, a known heretic, was seriously to sin. It was in fact to risk excommunication, as it was for a Catholic to be seen inside a Protestant church.

Personalities emerged in the telling, like Éamon de Valera, a towering figure who had occupied the stage almost continuously since the rebellion against the British in 1916, with his passionate aim for the uniting of the island, his skill as a negotiator, his success, in spite of outward pressures, in maintaining Ireland's neutrality during the war.

As I read on it seemed to me that the question should arise as to just how this inscrutable patriot of Spanish-American heritage had managed so successfully to steer his upward course and remain so firmly lodged on his pedestal, considering his rigid concern for the dominant role that Roman Catholic moral teaching should play in State affairs, and his seeming lack of such concern when it came to social progress, or consideration for religious minorities. Again, I was troubled by his mythical, almost Hitlerian, dream for Irish rural society where, instead of buxom, blond, blue-eyed Teutons thumping around dressed up as peasants, it was to be innocent, nimble-footed Gaels dancing jigs and reels, singing and conversing in a language which few but themselves could understand. As I turned the pages I found myself asking, as had possibly many others, if de Valera's reign had not been over-long and thus successfully retarded not only Ireland's ultimate unity, but also her advance into the twentieth century.

So many sins, so much wickedness, so many pastoral warnings — but I had spent twelve years of my life in a country where real wickedness ruled the land and I could only wonder at the triviality of such authoritarian rules and regulations designed to keep the people of Ireland on a straight and narrow, but utterly cheerless, path.

As for a once all-powerful Protestant minority, they seemed to have opted out, content to play no further role in public life, sending their sons to school in England, later perhaps to die for England and her causes.

But then my disquiet began to wane, for I only had to venture abroad to detect a certain philosophical attitude not only towards the laws of the land, but also to the constant priestly exhortations. There had to be tragedies lurking beneath the surface of such a rigid regime; poverty, ignorance, unwanted pregnancies, and heart-rending farewells. But when I saw the ordinary folk around us going about their daily business, coming from their prayers, their weddings, even their funerals, chatting and laughing, flirting and joking, they did not look overburdened with wickedness, nor for that matter particularly penitent; a state of affairs I could believe to be most frustrating for their prelates, but to me a great relief.

If I were occasionally inclined to despair at the seemingly endless wrangle between Church and State, when the battalions drawn up on the one side seemed too entrenched and on the other too supine, where hopes for a slight degree of social advancement were silenced again and again in the interest of ecclesiastical sanctity, I was given cause for further relief when I first experienced the Irish electoral system. The countryside was disfigured for weeks beforehand, and for months after-wards, by huge posters portraying would-be statesmen, doing their utmost to look purposeful, honest and reliable. Determined to become a loyal Irish citizen, I changed my passport once again to one emblazoned with the Irish harp. I was in no position to write them all off as did a fellow voter, from whom I sought advice on my way to the polling station. 'Sons of their dead Da's, publicans, and the rest – nothing but holy chancers' was my companion's summing-up, pushing his cap to the back of his head, with no sign of rancour, as we moved inside preparatory to playing our part in the shaping of the country's future.

On such occasions, a farm house up the road did duty as a Polling Station, and as I stood in the makeshift cabin set up in the parlour, pencil in hand, studying a list of names, none of which made sense to me, and listened to the rattling of tea cups from the kitchen next door where our local Garda – our arm of the law – was ensconced with some neighbours beside a cosy turf fire, my thoughts inevitably drifted back to the last time I recorded my vote in 1937. 'Heil Hitler, your name, please,' Nazi flags, brown shirts, pillbox hats, shining boots and clicking heels, and one blank square, just one, in which to express your opinion. *'Ja – Nein'*, 'Yes – No', and the eerie sensation that my hand holding the pencil was being very carefully studied by a pair of very attentive eyes.

So much for the history books and my amateur attempt to make head or tail of so much that was contradictory in the land in which we now lived. It could have been inertia, it could also have come from a certain sense of sadness which seemed to pervade those pages, but it was more likely the arrival of spring, when the days grew longer and one glorious sunrise after another lit up the eastern sky, which encouraged me to lay books aside, and turn to another source. It was a hidden source, nearer to home, more manageable, which as folk were dying, memories fading, and television and the motor car were fast invading the land, could soon be gone forever.

The facts had been carefully recorded in deeds and documents and meticulously confirmed by statistical survey. The lands of 'Munny' or 'Money', an anglicized version from the Gaelic *'Muine'*, to denote a copse, a group of trees, consisted of four hundred and fifty statute acres of Irish land not to be mistaken for Irish acres of a larger dimension. These were spurious measurements created by Cromwell when he parcelled out Irish land to his victorious soldiery. In 1949 they were still in use, but the reason for their usage had not been forgotten by the descendants of the dispossessed. These acres were now entrusted to us to do with as we willed. We could either allow the gorse and ferns to creep in further, and the rushes to advance at will, or see to it that each separate field be allowed to develop its own personality, changing its character from season to season, from year to year, to become a shifting patchwork of greens and golds.

I had my own kingdom and had not yet explored its

176

boundaries; The Rath, The Moate and the hidden corners sheltering ivy-covered ruins; *sibíní* or *tigíní*, small, tiny roofless homesteads where once big families were born and reared in bygone days.

I also had my historians to hand. Will Byrne, our herdsman, lived across the hill and had spent all his working life with the former owners of the land; he knew every hump and hollow of his kingdom. From him we learned that each field had its name. The Rathfield, with its scrap of circular scrubland and a blackthorn tree, insignificant enough if you were not in the know, but a certain sure landmark indicating what must be a ruined homestead beneath. His advice was, 'Best not to meddle with it' nor with the grassy hummock planted with tall trees and known as 'The Moate', a place of burial perhaps. 'Best not to meddle with that either,' for it was known that the souls of departed Druids sometimes took a notion to return to such places, and no luck would come the way of any temporary custodian who might think to tidy up, to flatten such hindrances, and thus cause the rightful original owners much inconvenience.

The Mistress's Bog – Miss Kitty's Grove – The Racecourse. Who was that unknown lady who gave her name to a windflower-covered swamp? Who was Miss Kitty, who must have wandered through her grove? Did she wander alone?

My informant was uncertain as to the identity of 'The Mistress', except for knowing that there was a time when, in years past, the Lord Fitzwilliam oft-times came to visit, and it was he who in old age installed the graceful staircase whose shallow steps were fashioned so that the mistress of the house, older now too and troubled with rheumatism, could ascend to her chamber nice and easy.

As for Miss Kitty, she was a poor one, gave her heart to a handsome local priest, and was only able to tell of her love by way of the confessional. The way it was, little notes passed back and forth by way of the dividing grid. All went well until one day it was a stranger who sat before her in the darkness, and it was he who received the scrap of paper and thought to tell his superiors of such an obvious mortal sin.

As Will took a long draw on his pipe, I was beginning to fear he was about to launch into another tragedy. Poor Miss Kitty could have had it, gone into a decline or whatever love-sick ladies did in those days, but luckily, not at all. It would seem a certain confusion set in here, as some said the priest was banished to another parish, others that he left straight away for America, but all were agreed that he returned to his Miss Kitty, and one dark night they left together, destination unknown. As neither of us could suppress happy smiles, I could gather that both Will and I were much content with this solution, he adding, 'God forgive them', just to make quite sure.

The Big Stone Field yielded up its full story when a local stonemason arrived in the yard telling me that he'd heard that the Boss Man wished to clear the land of some larger rocks using dynamite, and he'd come to make enquiries. After offering the usual opening remarks as to the weather which, in Ireland, is usually 'grand', 'soft', or 'barbarous', he hesitated before coming to the subject and then explained that the way it was when accepting the job, he had failed to ask Peter what he intended doing about the big stone in the Stone Field. 'Would the Boss Man be thinking of meddling with it?' was how he expressed himself, and, recognizing that key word, it was not difficult for me to reassure him about the big stone, as I was certain it would have needed all the dynamite in his possession to blow even a small hole in it. When he showed relief, and assured me he would be along the next morning, I could not help asking the reason for his initial hesitation. He seemed surprised at my ignorance, but was also very happy and willing to launch into his story, which, as he explained after first leading me to the front of the house, began on the heights of Aghold Hill before us. He presumed that I, of course, knew that St Kevin was often inclined to wander in the Wicklow Mountains, but maybe it was a new one on me that one day he stood up there with the wind to his back, threw his cloak in the air and called into the wind that where it fell to earth, there he would build his church. 'And the Holy Man kept his word,' said the stonemason, 'for there, can you not see, it still stands.'

For a moment I could not see why a small roofless church, built more than a thousand years ago, could have much to do with dynamite, but the stonemason was in full flight, caught up in the natural eloquence of his race.

'Centuries passed,' he said, 'and the Holy Man's little chapel became a meeting place for all those who would not desert the Faith and when a wee bell called them, they would flock along the Mass paths, the hidden ways, to worship before the altar of St Kevin. Then came one dark night, when the wind was again blowing strongly from the west, and the bell did toll no more. What would I say to that?' he asked, and I could only look at him expectantly, knowing that there was more to come. 'It was thieves, you see,' he said, 'and them dragging the bell over the fields, when a mighty flash lit up the sky and there was a powerful rumbling and they turned to see a rock break away from the hillside and come at them. And whichever way they turned and twisted, wheeled and stumbled, it came after them until they reached the field before us, and they could run no further, and they let loose the bell and fled, and the big stone rolled on and over it, and stopped where it is today.'

The stonemason had been pointing out the route taken by the thieves as if it had all happened last week and when his outstretched arm fell to his side, I thought he had come to the end of his tale, but — 'Every seven years, they do be saying — the old ones, that is — that they can hear the wee bell tolling and then if you have an ear for it, comes the rustling and the whispering along the Mass paths. I don't know, it may be so, it may not be so, but whichever way it is, I wouldn't meddle with it,' he concluded, as he bade me good day until the morrow.

The mystery as to why water came through the roof by the gallon had been easily solved; one Bangor slate was worth one bottle of Guinness, and our predecessors had preferred Guinness. Why I often shared my bath with a few tadpoles puzzled me quite a lot until, here again, Will Byrne came to the rescue when he told us of the Watercourse and what he called 'the grandeur of it'. Grand indeed had been its conception in the mid-nineteenth century; grand also the achievement of bringing water from the hills to flow for miles between cut granite banks in sufficient volume to move huge water wheels which drove the rugged machines which churned and chopped, thrashed and pulped the produce of the Munny Estate when it was in its heyday at the turn of the century.

Not so grand, I would say, for those smallholders who, for fear of eviction, laboured for a pittance in its construction, but who, had they known it, could bide their time awaiting the inevitable decline of their Protestant landlord's power over their lives. For as one Land Act followed another, and as the twentieth century progressed, a World War, a successful rebellion, and the declaration of an Irish Free State finally and successfully upset the former social structure of their island.

There were surely some landlords less profligate, less defeated, than our predecessors and perhaps it was too much to ask of former tenantry to show enthusiasm for an emblem of the past in which they had played little role except as under-dog. Nonetheless, when we took over with our hopes for the future, years of neglect had allowed the granite dykes to collapse into the water so that cattle could splash their way along the stream unheeded and an ingenious sluice gate used to control the flow had disappeared beneath a slimy green carpet of water weeds. At the end of the line the rusted water wheels with rotting flails now hung motionless on their axles.

Ireland, Ireland – burdened with so many abandoned projects, so many dilapidated grandeurs. On the upper reaches of the flow, the usual intrigues were soon to follow; fields flooded here, a sudden dearth there, and no one around on whom to lay the blame. For us at least, with the discovery of a well in the woods behind the house, the Watercourse and the 'grandeur of it' had come to its end and with it the tadpoles in the bath-tub.

Chapter Fourteen

I HAVE TOLD of those early years when Peter and I left his country in ruins behind us, and of how we turned a corner to find ourselves carrying on in uncharted territory.

We were not alone in our venture, for we had our three sons with us and for them holidays became sheer hard work. In spite of a few guaranteed flea bites, a visit to the local cinema was mind-blowing entertainment and two whole pound notes a month could be looked upon as a princely wage. Hedging, ditching, stooking, stacking, the daily slog when farming the land; Peter and his 'Four-Year Plan' would have been hard put without their loyal involvement.

Progress, progress, cattle and sheep, more cattle, more sheep, hardly any debts, and in spite of dire warnings that only oats could ever prosper on our exhausted Munny lands, Peter had signed a contract with Messrs Guinness to grow barley, considered at the time to be a far more lucrative crop.

In those days no local farmer had learned to apply limestone to acid soil such as ours and soon many a cautious neighbour could be seen leaning over our gates watching for the emergence of that first crop of barley, until one day it was once more Will Byrne who could finally declare that whatever Peter was putting into his 'bag stuff' the crop was growing apace and looked like surviving. Limestone was a key which had obviously unlocked an infinite supply of unused fertility and Peter's much groaned about 'Four-Year Plan' with Stephen Cullinan's and Paddy Dawson's enthusiastic co-operation had come of age and laid the foundation for what looked like becoming a flourishing enterprise.

The farming cycle maintains a slow inevitable rhythm all of its own – the ploughing, the sowing, the greening and ripening finally reaching a climax, the crest of the wave, on that final day of the harvest when after the crows, the rabbits and the weather have all been defied, the gate can be closed on that very last field to be cleared of its crop.

It is hard to describe the jubilant sense of accomplishment which follows that ultimate trailer load of corn as it trundles off down the road heading for the loft, the silo or the corn merchant.

The harvesting days in Munny were unusual, maybe even unique, for our sons were joined each year by a team of extra hands (almost able to lay claim to being a miniature community of nations). They were the sons and daughters of friends and relatives, particularly from England and Germany, but also from France and Italy and as far afield as Botswana – Christian and Otto, Fritz, Elke, Pierre and Winfried, Leapeetswe and Sekgoma, their goal was doubtless to learn English but language seemed no barrier as they rode the tractors, lugged and loaded the sacks or relaxed together leaning up against the banks and hedgerows.

My particular role in the harvest ritual was to 'bring up the tea'. On hearing that the activity in the field might go on well into the night, I would then appear at 6 o'clock with my equally international retinue of 'home-helps' and enough sustenance to keep things going for a few more hours; Puppi and Angela, Verena and Adi, Renate and Rixi, and as I had long decided that I must be one of the least-efficient housewives in the business, I could only hope their mothers had not expected that, besides English, under my tutelage they might also pick up a few hints as to how a large household should be run.

I do not remember, however, that a lack of confidence was ever one of my failings, and so as the sun disappeared behind the hills and the mugs of tea and doorstep sandwiches did the rounds, I could sit back with them amongst the bulging sacks listening to their laughter and their cheerful misuse of the English language and think that maybe this journey to Ireland was giving these children something more important. They belonged to a new generation unburdened by impending war as we had been, and hopefully could remain undisturbed by race or colour, never again having even to contemplate sallying forth to kill each other.

As the years flowed by, I learned, too, that a certain pattern seems to emerge in the life of a family. In the beginning two people, strangers to each other so far, meet by chance and joyfully set off on a journey together, as yet unaware of what lies ahead of them. When children join the scene they set a family routine in motion – nursery days – school days – university – and suddenly, they are no longer children but, grown to adulthood, are off and away as is their right. One hopes that the family ties will remain intact, but close family involvement in their affairs inevitably loosens. In practical terms the family bank account looks far more cheerful, but the landscape without those loved landmarks lies curiously deserted.

I learned that it had to be, but did not find it easy to cast aside a protective role and accept that children belong to the future, a tomorrow country filled with surprises, adventure and also suffering as it had been for me when I left England for Germany so many years before. Fortunately the hiatus in our family did not last for too long. A year, two years or so, then came the grandchildren, and prams and cots and teddy bears could re-emerge from retirement to take up their duties once again. Nor was I destined to spend too long moping about the place, sadly aware of favourite haunts deserted and prize possessions abandoned; a tree house in the woods, an old bag of golf clubs, even a stray pair of football boots proving sometimes enough to set me off.

I was freed of such attacks of nostalgia when I heard from David Astor that a plan was afoot for a British author to produce a biography on the life of Adam von Trott, whose effort to hinder the outbreak of war in 1939 and to convince the British government of a German opposition to Hitler had proved to no avail.

Adam had been a Rhodes scholar at Oxford during the 1930s and my mandate was to help the author by conducting some research into that period of his life. I was glad to do so for Adam had been a close friend of ours during the war; in fact it was he, an ardent anti-Nazi, who persuaded us not to emigrate to Ireland in 1938, but to join with him and others in opposition to Hitler and his regime.

On my return to England I had heard rumours that his failure to convince had come about because doubts as to his *bona fides* had been circulated by former university contemporaries. Many of them had since become eminent scholars in their various fields and unfortunately their voices had been listened to.

Germany had nothing to be proud of during Hitler's reign, but there were two outstanding exceptions. Firstly, the courage and tenacity of her soldiers when, inadequately equipped, they ultimately found themselves defending their country against the whole world. Secondly, the 20th July Bomb Plot, when those who had taken part so nearly succeeded in ridding their country of a monster who had ruled over them for eleven years and who claimed their lives when it failed.

Unlike the British, the Germans I found were slow to honour their real heroes. I often had to think of those tattered, shattered remains of the mighty German army whom I had seen in 1945 in Frankfurt, squatting on the pavements, sheltering in doorways with their begging bowls beside them, and found myself comparing their plight with that of the British Expeditionary Force which was given such a joyous heartwarming welcome when, equally defeated, they returned home to England from France in 1940. Different, so different, and it seemed to me not only appropriate, but rather typical, that Adam's heroic story should be one of the first to be told in English by an English author.

I had not been back to Oxford since my 'deb' days in 1929, somehow not daring to do so in case this very beautiful seat of learning might shake my resolve to abandon a scholarship and to study music in Germany instead.

As I proceeded from one noble precinct, one interview, one thimbleful of sherry to the next, it became clear that as a student in Balliol, three years older than themselves, Adam had played a dramatic role in many of these people's lives. Although only one learned scholar admitted to remorse at having spread false rumours, not one could understand why Adam had not trusted their friendship and come clean as to his true attitude to Nazism. In 1959 I spent ten days listening, trying and failing to explain how impossible this would have been if he wished to return to his country. As it was, news of my own humble arrival was already busy doing the rounds of this cloistered community, and friendship or no friendship, I could easily calculate just how long Adam's possible confession as to his true political thinking would have taken to reach official Nazi ears.

By the time my visit came to an end I realized that by wishing to help an author I had gone a long way to clearing my own mind. Intellectual achievement, I decided, rests on very narrow and immature emotional foundations. To study history was an intellectual exercise; to live it was beyond my listeners' comprehension. No one could understand what it was like to live under a dictatorship unless they had experienced it themselves.

Before leaving, I had just one more interview to complete, this time with a noted don, and an historian I much admired. After I had delivered my usual impassioned earful he remarked quietly, 'Well, my dear, it looks to me as if there is a missing book. If you feel so strongly about it, why don't you write it yourself?'

The train journey back to London passed quickly because, in spite of the pile of notes I had collected for my mission, I knew that the final interview had been for me the most momentous. When the train jolted to a halt in Paddington Station I had made up my mind to accept the challenge.

I was staying with my mother at the time who, to escape the loneliness of my father's death, had moved to a little house near to my elder brother in St John's Wood, and always came to us in Ireland for the summer months. When I burst in on her, bringing with me my newly discovered ambition, I was surprised, almost overcome, by the instant enthusiasm with which she greeted what could still be a pipe dream.

Her own literary efforts had never reached much beyond an occasional postcard; potent enough postcards though, giving her advice in the briefest possible terms, but conveying also how often she had helped us ride out the storm financially: 'Let's go a bust and get an Aga', 'Hope the new harvester is doing its stuff', 'Love to Peter and thanks for cheque'. In her day, as she often explained, education was reserved for sons, and she was the youngest of the Harmsworth clan with eleven brothers lined up ahead of her. Her particular determined personality saw to it, however, that she more than held her own. In a day or so she had a room upstairs ready for me, equipped with a writing table, pencils and paper. Whenever I should be in London the order of the day was to leave me in peace.

For some years peace was not the word I would have chosen to describe my state of mind for it meant confronting sad memories packed neatly away in a corner of the mind and not to be disturbed with comfort. There were some days when words seemed to flow faster than a pen could cover the paper, and others when the well ran dry, the page remained a blank, and I just wished that some celestial being would float in and tell me firmly that enough was enough. The only such being whose judgement I felt I could trust was my cousin, Cecil King, who rang me up after reading the first two chapters and let me know in true Cecil fashion that if I did not continue he would never speak to me again.

It is a long and harrowing journey until the moment comes when the publisher hands you back your story which has miraculously become a book with its pages neatly bound and its cover decked out, ready to face the world. It was 1968 before Ian Parsons of Chatto & Windus, after apologizing for a delay which had occurred in its production, handed it to me most gently, almost lovingly, and said, 'Here it is at last, dear Chris, and if I may say so it is my opinion that we may have a classic in our hands.'

The delay in publishing saddened me for I had much hoped that my mother could have shared in its possible success. It was not to be, for she died shortly before the publication. It did not seem fair, for I could not tell her that when it came to choosing a title I had needed help, and that, when sorting forlornly through her possessions, I came across her little Victorian Birthday Book; birthdays of family and friends had been faithfully recorded and to each date belonged a small quotation from the works of Robert Louis Stevenson. I turned instinctively to a date which meant as much to me as many a birthday – 20th July – and the quotation beneath from Stevenson's *Tales of the Road* read: 'The future is nothing, but the past is myself, my own history, the seed of my present thoughts, the mould of my present disposition.'

The Past is Myself, my book had its title, and I was comforted because in a roundabout way I felt my mother's clear voice had not yet been stilled.

Epilogue

ONE OF THE many problems confronting anyone who has decided to risk writing an auto-biography must be to decide when that life story should be allowed to reach a certain conclusion. In simple terms, to know very definitely where and when to stop. If your life happens to have been eventful a further problem must arise as to what should be included and what left out.

I could and should have told more of Leapeetswe and Sekgoma Khama, who dropped in for three days on their way to school in Ireland and stayed for four years – Peachy and Secky, 'the two black lads' as they came to be known to the townsfolk of Tullow – and of the letter Peachy wrote to me after his father died and he had to leave Trinity College to return to Botswana and take his place as paramount chief of his tribe. 'Madre' – by then we had adopted each other and I was very sad to see my black lad go – 'Madre,' he wrote, 'you cannot know what it is like to have the door to knowledge opened a small way and then slammed shut.'

I could have told of the Peace Rallies and of how one day we all arrived with our banners on the southern bank of the River Boyne, and the silence we met with until a sea-mist lying over the river lifted – and they were there, the Northern women in equal numbers – and the cries of joy which greeted us as we flooded across the bridge. Laughter, hugs and kisses, a heartwarming welcome and agreement later over endless cups of tea that it was surely nonsense to allow men to run the affairs of the world.

Maybe I should have told of my association with the Peace People, and their charismatic leaders, Betty Williams and Mairead Corrigan, of my experience and growing admiration for the sturdy self-reliance of those other Northern women, and of my enthusiasm after joining those rallies when women from the North and South of Ireland crossed the divide together and convinced me that if peace and ceasing of bloodshed were to come to this small divided island it would be brought about by the women.

Then if my ambition was to provide a grand finale, what could be more dramatic than finding myself in the Great Hall, the Aula Maxima of Heidelberg University, perched on a platform with Betty Williams by my side? My role was to be that of interpreter, but although the hall was crowded it did not look as if we were to have much success with our peace message. As soon as Betty opened her mouth she was greeted by howling groups of well-trained rowdies, obviously made in Germany, whose chorused protests amounted to yells of, 'Up ze Repoblik' and 'Get ze Brits out of Doblin.'

The police were moving in to our rescue when Betty stepped down from the platform, approached one of the ringleaders, took him firmly by the shoulders, plonked him on a chair and announced in clarion tones, 'Sit there, 'till I tell ye to get up. I'm going to speak and you're going to listen, d'y hear me, y' wee fucker!' From then on the stupefied yob sat transfixed while Betty returned to continue her piece to a silent, spellbound audience. I sat beside her doing my stuff, relieved that no interpreter had been needed to translate that particular piece of good, sound Belfast rhetoric.

After some thought I finally decided that I would shut

up shop, close the shutters, in the summer of 1979 when I celebrated my seventieth birthday.

There are one or two advantages in reaching the age of seventy when still more or less in right mind. Not many I would say, just one or two.

Firstly perhaps that with luck you have reached a comforting conclusion that to forget certain happenings and events is so usual that for one's peace of mind it is best taken for granted. Then, a certain leaning towards eccentricity is permissible and most of the time looked upon with tolerant amusement.

It need not go so far as a charming old lady I encountered one day when the two of us were looking in a window of Harrods. She was wearing a neat little toque and a short fur jacket with a scrap of some animal about her neck which used to be known as a tippet. I spoke to her because I felt that someone should let her know that she had forgotten to put on her skirt. 'Thank you, my dear, thank you,' she said showing no sign of embarrassment. 'In that case perhaps I had better make for home.'

There are also what might be called tricks of the trade, as I learned when wedged between two senior citizens on a flight between Dublin and Heathrow. My neighbours were two cheerful old ladies who had obviously travelled extensively, for they were soon chatting of Hong Kong, Australia, the Caribbean, as if such places were just around the corner. It was also obvious that the paraphernalia of travel, the complexities involved in the crossing of national frontiers left them undaunted, for they were loaded down with duty-free goods and seemed to have plenty of baggage in the hold. Both were agreed that an air of helplessness was essential if fellow travellers were to be encouraged to show more than usual consideration, or for officialdom a benevolent side to their nature.

'Everyone is so kind,' beamed the one. 'And I haven't been caught once!' boasted the other.

As we downed our whiskies together the lady to my right admitted to having occasionally gone to the extreme of putting one arm into a sling and that she always carried one with her — 'just in case' — but she to my left declared that she found a slight limp and a walking-stick to be quite sufficient.

As I listened, fascinated by their exploits, I began to believe in the existence of some kind of Mafia designed exclusively for oldies. In fact it only needed a second whisky before I found little harm in such behaviour and my initial unease turned to admiration. After all, it is not so long ago that elderly ladies were expected to wear constant mourning and to live in the hope of finding someone to push them around in a bath chair. Instead, my companions were off and away defying old age, bent on enjoying themselves and filled with warm appreciation of human nature at its best.

So, to my own birthday; 18th June to be exact. It was a date I could easily remember, not only because I arrived in the world on that midsummer's day in 1909, but because the Battle of Waterloo was won on the same day in 1815.

It happened that one of the earlier arguments I had with Peter concerned that particular battle, because at school our history teacher, doubtless a true patriot, had provided me with the rather puzzling piece of information that this great British victory was 'fought and won on the playing fields of Eton'. Peter, however, could only remember from his history class that as the battle dragged on Wellington prayed, 'Would that it were eve and the Prussians were here.' And sure enough they arrived in the nick of time. So much for history lessons; a timely warning to both of us when we were trying to feel our way towards a deeper understanding between our two countries.

Now, half a century later, with the exploding of many such national myths behind us, our family had multiplied to include daughters-in-law and a host of grandchildren, and they were of the opinion that as I was the first amongst them to arrive at such a venerable plateau, just one party to celebrate my Seventieth would not be enough. In their enthusiasm they decided that the festivities should last a whole weekend commencing in Munny on the evening of the day before. This, being Ireland, was an assurance that they would continue until long after midnight and last well on into my birthday. Then, if I was still able for it, a dinner party would take place in a nearby schoolhouse which had been skilfully converted into a restaurant. Due to an abundance of 'acceptances with pleasure' the home celebrations would perforce have to overflow into the garden. Seeing that it had rained ceaselessly for weeks beforehand this seemed to me a particularly brave decision.

But now the prospects did not look so dire. In spite of those weeks of so-called 'soft weather', the forecasters had stuck their necks out far enough to predict that a ridge of high pressure developing even into an anti-cyclone might be making its way towards us across the Atlantic. For once they proved right, for on the day before our own particular 'hooley' was to take place, the hills emerged from behind their clouds, the mists drifted away down the valley and the sun rose at dawn to move warmly across a cloudless sky until one of Ireland's miraculous sunsets set the western sky ablaze.

Such unexpected good fortune galvanized everyone around me into immediate action. Peter, off to Kilmore Quay to fetch lobsters; Heather, a daughter-in-law, with Cis, my faithful housekeeper, and Elke, a good friend, to start preparing the cold buffet supper; grandchildren to set about mowing the lawns and clipping the hedges; my brother John from Switzerland who, having cast his expert eye over my dishevelled flowerbeds, to decide that what he called 'instant gardening' was the only solution. This involved his making tracks for the nearest garden centre to equip himself with shrubs and plants in full flower. Not exactly the Sissinghurst routine perhaps, but the result, he assured us, would be electrifying. The instructions given to me by my family and friends were to relax and do nothing.

So it happened that, with plenty of hustle and bustle going on around me, I found myself sitting alone on a deck-chair in the sun; alone with my thoughts and my years in what had once been my vegetable garden until I gave up the unequal struggle with slugs and weeds and we went berserk and installed a swimming-pool.

The swimming-pool garden then, a quiet green place now, with just the pool and the lawn surrounded by grey stone walls covered with rambling roses. A thick laurel hedge to one side protected it from the north winds which could blow in from the Wicklow Mountains. Very quiet, very green, and as I sat there in the peace, the warmth and the silence, I found my thoughts wandering away on their own.

Thirty-three years had slipped by since I stood leaning on a low wall in Kilmore Quay looking out over the sea to the Saltee Islands. Small waves were lapping at the rocks below me and the cry of many seagulls rang in my ears as they followed the fishing boats out to the fishing grounds. On that day I had come to a tentative conclusion to live out my days if possible in this beautiful and unpredictable island. And this we had done, whilst Peter built up what was now considered to be a flourishing farm. Munny House, too, had become a home and, to judge from those who had travelled far to be with us this weekend, a home for many besides ourselves. Children of those who had been killed by Hitler, coming for the holidays and always returning; our own sons growing up here, married now, and nine grandchildren. I would like to think that Peter and I had managed to build something on the ruins we had left behind us. Something perhaps demanded of us by the very fact that we had survived. I would like to believe that we had provided a centre, a never-changing reality which they could look back upon and hold in their hearts with happiness as they grew up to face an ever-changing world.

Ireland, too, had changed in those thirty-three years. Ireland now had television, Ireland had supermarkets. Ass-carts and horse-drawn tinkers' caravans were now only there for the tourists, for Ireland now had motor cars, and Virgin Marys and teddy bears no longer bobbed about in their rear windows 'just in case'. Perhaps the peak of modern convenience known as 'family planning' had not yet reached the statute books, but there was always the possibility of slipping across the Irish Sea in order to stock up or, if need be, avoid the consequences. The birthrate was not quite what it used to be, dear God, so it wasn't.

A breath of wind rustled the leaves of the copper-beech tree which overhung the garden and a swallow swooped over me, skimmed the surface of the pool and shot up to join a group of its frolicking companions. The swallows had returned to their nests in the rafters early this year, and they were flying high. Another good omen for the weather to come.

I tried to concentrate on the only task allotted to me which was to decide on the seating arrangements for the dinner to take place on the following day. A carefully prepared list of participants had been thrust into my hand and I had shown a degree of enthusiasm to be of help at least in some small way. But now with my eye running down from one name to the next, David Astor, Sekgoma Khama, Betty Williams, I found myself wondering was it so important where they sat themselves down? They knew each other after all, would fit themselves in anywhere, each in their own way slipping without fuss into their allotted place in the jigsaw pattern of my life.

The sun was high and warm above me and the shape of my chair becoming more congenial by the minute, so that I suspected that it would not be long before I fell asleep.

I have never discovered the exact moment when sleep and dreams take over from reality. As a child I could tell more or less, because of the advent too often of an ever-recurring nightmare. Myself very small and alone surrounded by a huge and silent emptiness until distant walls began to close in around me and as they moved in nearer I could hear voices, many voices, increasing in volume until the chattering became strident screeching. It was then, when I could bear it no longer, that I usually awoke screaming equally noisily and in need of much comfort.

Today I would doubtless have been taken to visit a psychiatrist, but in those days the explanation given was that I must have eaten something for supper which had disagreed with me and if I wished to avoid a dose of castor oil I would have to find my own solution. I did so one night when I turned on those threatening walls and burst out laughing. To my joy they were silenced immediately. They were defeated and I awoke with a childlike conviction that horrors cannot survive ridicule.

A passer-by could be forgiven if he thought to recognize an elderly lady comfortably ensconced in the sun, hands folded in lap, eyes closed, just about to nod off. But Christabel was not asleep, at least she did not think she was, although it was certainly a little odd to find that she was no longer alone in her garden and that the granite, rose-covered walls seemed to have melted away into the woodlands behind them, where oak trees had become conifers; giant Christmas trees swaying and sighing in the wind as they had done in the Black Forest when they freed themselves from the winter snows.

Nor was this all, for there was movement in the depths of the woods and she could hear voices. They were not strident human cacklings as in her childhood, but friendly gentle sounds and there was laughter in the air.

Had there been some mention of a birthday party? Could it be about to start? She tried to stand up and move towards a colourful throng, a sudden sparkling river which seemed to flow towards her out of the shadows into the sunlight. But she could not stir, could not join them. It was as if she were rooted to the earth and could only watch silently as one familiar being after another passed her by. Her father, her mother, a much-loved brother, Freda, Adam, Lexi, Frau Muckle – this was no ordinary gathering, these were never-to-be-forgotten people, their faces as clear and as dearly loved as when they left her years back to travel along the rest of her road without them.

Splash – a sound like a pistol shot rang out and echoed through my head, shattering the silence, scattering my dream people. I awoke with a start to find myself staring over the edge of the swimming-pool into the laughing face of – could it be my son? – no, it must be my grandson. Why is it that in photographs people are always smiling, in dreams they never grow old? 'I'm sorry, Chris,' he said, turning and diving like a dolphin to reappear at the far end of the pool and call back, 'Please don't ever be seventy again, Grandma, your lawns look super, but I'm pooped!'

Whereupon he proceeded to thresh up and down the pool at what to me seemed almost the speed of sound. I could not help smiling at his effort to belie his state of exhaustion and stood watching him for a while for he was surely showing off a bit too, which I knew to be no fun at all unless someone is there looking on.

On rounding the corner of the house I could hear the bees busily working away under the slates of the roof. They had been there for several years now and there must be gallons of honey awaiting anyone who was willing to risk dismantling part of the house.

Before going indoors I stood for a short while on the steps before the front door, newly painted for the occasion, and looked about me. There were sheep grazing half-heartedly in the lawn field, and down in the valley a drifting pool of sunlight picked out St Kevin's little roofless ivy-covered church. I was only going to be seventy after all, but watched over by the rounded heather-covered hills of Aghold and Aghade, it had braved the elements for seven centuries.

Maybe there was something uncanny in the sultry air; perhaps my strange dream still held me in its spell for, as I stood there, looking about me, able to recognize every hill and hollow, for a moment in time it seemed to me that I now belonged to those hills and they to me for ever – in eternity.

So it was that, a little off-balance, but still eager to be of some help, I retreated into the cool welcoming half-light of the house.